WORDS YOU **THOUGHT** YOU KNEW . . .

1001 Commonly Misused
and Misunderstood Words and Phrases

by Jenna Glatzer

ADAMS MEDIA
Avon, Massachusetts

Published by
Adams Media, an F+W Publications Company
57 Littlefield Street, Avon, MA 02322. U.S.A.
www.adamsmedia.com

ISBN: 1-58062-941-5

Printed in Canada.

J I H G F E D C B A

Library of Congress Cataloging-in-Publication Data
Glatzer, Jenna.
Words you thought you knew / Jenna Glatzer.
p.   cm.
ISBN 1-58062-941-5
1. English language--Usage--Dictionaries. 2. English language--Terms
and phrases. 3. Vocabulary. I. Title.

PE1464.G55 2003
428'.003--dc21
2003006180

This publication is designed to provide accurate and authoritative information with regard to the subject matter covered. It is sold with the understanding that the publisher is not engaged in rendering legal, accounting, or other professional advice. If legal advice or other expert assistance is required, the services of a competent professional person should be sought.
—From a *Declaration of Principles* jointly adopted by a
Committee of the American Bar Association and a
Committee of Publishers and Associations

Many of the designations used by manufacturers and sellers to distinguish their products are claimed as trademarks. Where those designations appear in this book and Adams Media was aware of a trademark claim, the designations have been printed with initial capital letters.

This book is available at quantity discounts for bulk purchases.
For information, call 1-800-872-5627.

Gale Kennedy, Diane Mayor Kniffin, Mridu Khullar, Beth Kujawski, Lisa LaRue, John LaVine, Star Lawrence, Lucy Lewis, Jack Lugar, Alfred P M, Andrea L. Mack, Steve MacKenzie, Denise Mainquist, Corinne Malta, Tim Mattson, Vanessa McDaniel, Jacqueline McMahon, Karl Miller, Lisa Mitchell, Heidi R. Moore, Karina Moore, Betsy Morris, Phyllis Moses, Marli Murphy, Kathleen Myers, Sue Nussbaum, Mim Oaks, Amy Outland, Barbara Parks, Kaye Patchett, Linda Patterson, Leticia Araujo Perez, Sam AJ Pillay, Dawn C. Pitsch, Doug Powers, Mark Prindle, Shaunna Privratsky, Victor K. Pryles, LeAnn R. Ralph, Lydia Ramsey, Annie Rasiak, Mark L. Redmond, Jon Reischel, Eunice K. Riemer, Michael Riley, Leticia Rivera, Bill Roebuck, Sandra Rosinski, Mary J. Schirmer, Beth Schmidt, Valerie Schneider, Cora Scott, Barbara Sharpe, Anne Skalitza, Starla Sloan, Susan Stephenson, Roger Suchy, Katy Terrega, Lauren Teton, Alma Thompson, Sandy Thompson, Janis Thornton, Linda Thorpe, Argyro Toumazou, Janet West, Daniel Will-Harris, Glenda Williams, Jay Williams, Mindy Wilson, JoAnna Wool, and Jessica Wright.

A special thanks to Mary J. Schirmer for all of her help with the humor in this book and to Lawrence Benedict for going above and beyond the call of duty with his helpful e-mails.

And thank you to everyone at Adams Media, particularly my editors, Tracy Quinn McLennan and Courtney Nolan, for choosing me to write this book.

Acknowledgments

I'd like to thank all of the people who suggested words and phrases for inclusion in this book. Thanks to Sharon Agassi, Ed Allen, Cynthia Amorese, Amy Ashley, Carol Baier, Phil Barber, Laraine A. Barker, Lawrence Benedict, Howard Binkow, Craig Bloomfield, Julie Boehme, Mary M. Boldish, Amy Brozio-Andrews, Petrea Burchard, Alana Marie Burke, Dawn Caceres, John Carroll, Mary Case (I miss you), Carol Celeste, Tiffany Chepul, Bobbie Christmas, Dan Church, Steve Circeo, Christine Clouse, Victoria Congema, Mary Coyne, Donna D'Amour, Linda Dewey, Charles Dowdell, Susan C. Finelli, Scott Flanders, Peggy Forsberg, Patricia Fraser, Bernadette Geyer, Linda M. Gigliotti, Ed Gilhuly, Janice Goulart, Charmaine Greenwood, Liza Gutierrez-O'Neill, Mary Anne Hahn, Jane Hallisey, Jan Hallson, Mark Halpern, Jerry Hatchett, Graham Hayman, Melodee Heberden, Joyce Henderson, Jennifer Herrin, Mary Hightower, Jim Horn, Robin Hyman, Kathy Jones, Marie Karns, Roberta Kedzierski, Susan Kelly,

Dedication

This is dedicated to my wonderful English and writing teachers through the years, especially my mom, Carene Mahoney, Eric McHenry, and Professor Klipstein.

And it's dedicated to Anthony, the man who buys me chocolate coconut doughnuts when I'm on a writing bender.

Contents

Introduction

I'm the daughter of an English teacher. Perhaps it comes as no surprise, then, that I have a profound respect for language. I hate to see it abused and misconstrued, and I'm pretty hard on myself when I find out I've committed linguistic brutality.

That's not to say I don't make mistakes; I make them with alarming frequency, and what's worse is that I make them in public—roughly 62,000 writers subscribe to my Absolute Write newsletters (*www.absolutewrite.com*). They're a tough audience; whenever I make a gaffe in print, I can count on receiving dozens of e-mails that turn my cheeks an appropriate shade of red. I was chastised for including an ad that promised "50% off of our normal advertising rates," and nearly hanged when I wrote, "Mastery is mostly comprised of habit."

That's why I turned to them when I began this book. I asked those 62,000 writers to tell me which words and phrases they'd heard misused, and which words and phrases they'd heard but never completely understood, or never bothered to look up.

Boy, did I get responses, as you might have guessed if you looked at my acknowledgments page. My inbox was flooded with letters from writers who were eager to have a forum for their pet peeves. They told me about the words their bosses continually misconstrue, the phrases their friends mangle, and the words politicians never get right. And, voilà! This book was born.

We don't have a high literary council to determine the acceptable meanings of words, and, therefore, sources may disagree about "proper" definitions. In some cases, I may disagree with what your dictionary says, because dictionaries are generally descriptive rather than prescriptive (which means that they record the way the public uses words, without passing judgment about whether the usages are proper or not). Your mother may disagree with me. But what follows are my carefully considered thoughts on the matter of proper usage, the result of several months of research. Feel free to break my "rules," but now you'll have more information on which to base your opinions.

Ours is a living language, and as such, the accepted definitions of words can and do change over time. I suspect that certain words I'm about to define—such as *aggravate*—will eventually succumb to the public's misuse. A hundred years from now, literate folk may consider me a pedant for trying to hold on to the past and keep the traditional definitions pure. But does that stop me? No! I'm here to fight the good fight and keep you concerned readers "in the know" about words you may want to think about more carefully next time you employ them.

That's why you're here, I assume. You're a careful writer and/or speaker, and you want to get your words right. Well, good for you. The more of us there are, the more likely it is that we can stop misused and nonstandard words from becoming standard. I don't know about you, but if I see *irregardless* earn itself an unchallenged place in dictionaries, it'll be a day full of sighs and trudging for me.

I hope you enjoy the read, and I hope you'll have several "I never knew that" moments, as I did while I was reading through the e-mails. Thanks for picking up this book!

Words

Aa

a lot/allot/alot
Alot is not a standard word. If you want to say you have quite a bit, say you have *a lot*. Don't get lazy on me; you don't need to make *a lot* any shorter than it already is! The word *allot* means to ration out or designate for a purpose.

> *There are a lot of doughnuts left in my box.*

> *We have allotted two bottles of wine for Harry, and three bottles for the rest of our guests.*

a while *see* awhile

abbreviation/acronym
Initials only form an *acronym* if they make a word that can be pronounced. For example, the band All Styles Wicked sometimes goes by its initials, ASW. You can't pronounce "asw," so that's not an acronym. It is an *abbreviation*. Abbreviations are shortened forms of words or phrases. However, the

ab...

organization Drug Abuse Stops Here goes by its initials—
DASH—and Mothers Against Drunk Driving goes by
MADD. Those are acronyms.

"Etc." is an abbreviation for "etcetera."

"WOW" is an acronym for "Women Opposed to Waxing."

aberrant/abhorrent

If something is *aberrant*, it's different from the norm, usually
in a bad way, though it's not necessarily horrifying. *Aberrant*
has the same kind of ring as *deviant*. If it's *abhorrent*, it's
worthy of disgust or inspires feelings of detestation.

*Because of the boy's aberrant behavior, the teacher sent
him to the school psychologist.*

I find his nose-picking abhorrent.

abjure/adjure

Both of these verbs carry an air of solemnity. *Adjure* means to
command or earnestly urge. *Abjure* means to formally renounce,
as under oath.

*The police officer adjured the man to tell the truth about
why he was in a tree and holding binoculars.*

*He abjured his "die-hard bachelor" status on the day he
proposed.*

abscond

To *abscond* is to run off and hide, typically to avoid arrest or punishment. You'll often hear that someone has absconded with something (like jewels or money). That's incorrect because it means that the thing (the jewels, the money) has run off and hidden as well.

She took the stapler and absconded from the office.

accept/except

The word *accept* has several meanings: to deal with, to agree with, to consent to, to take, to include in a group, to believe in, or to acquiesce. (Versatile word, that *accept*!) *Except* means aside from; minus.

I have learned to accept that I'm never going to look good in a bikini.

Except James, who complained about having to wear shoes that the entire neighborhood has worn at one time or another, everyone had a good time at the bowling alley.

accidental/incidental

Something *accidental* happens unexpectedly or unintentionally, whereas something *incidental* is a relatively small thing that happens in accordance with something of larger importance. People sometimes misuse the word *incidentally* to introduce a big question or statement; for example, "Incidentally, didn't

George die in a car accident?" Pity poor George for his death having become so trivial. Only use *incidentally* when your topic is of little importance, such as "Incidentally, I forgot to pick up cereal at the grocery store."

It was accidental that she blurted out her pregnancy news while her busybody coworker was within earshot.

I had some incidental expenses when I got a new girlfriend.

acute/chronic

These two words are nearly opposite, yet they're often confused. *Acute* means "to come on quickly and sharply, but to last a short time"; *chronic* means long-lasting and constant or frequently recurring. *Chronic* can also mean *habitual* in contexts like "he is a chronic liar" or "she's a chronic complainer."

I got an acute headache when my kids started their "he touched me first" war.

I finally found out that my chronic abdominal pains were the result of eating nachos for breakfast every morning.

adherence/adhesion

Adhesion and *adherence* both mean the ability to stick to something or to stay attached, but it is preferable to use *adhesion* when you're referring to an object, and *adherence* when you're referring to a person.

When I was trying to superglue my broken vase, I accidentally touched my face and now I have a problem with my finger's adhesion to my cheek.

His adherence to the "no alcohol on campus" rule came as a big surprise to me because I once saw him sneak a beer into church.

adjacent

Did you know that, to be adjacent, things need to be similar? "*Adjacent* refers to *like* things that may or may not be in close contact," says Janice Goulart, editor of *The Telfair Enterprise*. "For example, farmhouses may be adjacent even though they are three miles apart if there are no other *like* things (farmhouses) in between. Another example: Someone may say the street is adjacent to the park. This is incorrect, as the street and park are not *like* things. It would be more correct to say 'the street runs past the park.'"

Even though we were engaged, we slept in adjacent rooms at my conservative parents' house.

adjure *see* abjure

adorable

Adorable means worthy of being adored. It's not another word for *cute*. Your teddy bear may be cute, but is it really worthy of adoration?

He is adorable because he risked his life to save a dog.

adverse/averse

The tricky part of these words is that people are not *adverse* to things, no matter how many times you hear that they are. People may be *averse* to something—that means they are opposed to it or strongly dislike it. *Adverse* means unfavorable, or serving to oppose.

The hog-calling competition was postponed because of adverse weather conditions.

I am averse to having any part of my body waxed.

advice/advise

Advice is a noun. *Advise* is a verb. Sounds simple enough, doesn't it? Yet I still get e-mails from people asking for my "advise" about how to become a writer. I tell them to start by learning the difference between *advice* and *advise*. (Then I advise them to buy my books. Not that I'm biased. Or mercenary.)

She never heeds my advice; that's why she married a lout.

She advised me to keep my mouth shut about the fact that I think her husband is a lout.

aerobics

People think you have to go to a gym in a spandex outfit and jump up and down to dance music to be doing aerobics. Actually, *aerobics* just means any activity that increases your oxygen intake. If you dance, walk, run, swim, or play soccer, you're doing aerobics.

After doing aerobics by running around the reservoir, I like to sit on the couch, watch television for eight hours, and eat cupcakes.

affect/effect

I'll admit that this one can be a little tricky. It would be easier if I could just tell you that *affect* is always a verb and *effect* is always a noun. But I can't. I can tell you that that's how it usually goes, but there are a few exceptions. *Effect* can be a transitive verb that means bring about or cause to be, as in "The teacher wanted to effect change," and in the psychological field, *affect* refers to a patient's facial expression. But for the most part, *affect* is a verb and *effect* is a noun.

Sitting on Santa's lap seemed to affect my son badly; he cried all the way home.

Watering the plants had a good effect on them; maybe I should remember to do it more often.

agape/agog

These two don't have much to do with each other, and yet, I've heard them get mixed up. Your mouth can't be *agog*. Come to think of it, if your mouth is *agape*, you're being redundant anyway. If you are *agape*, it means your mouth is open (denoting surprise), and if you're *agog*, you're very excited. In Christianity, *agape* (pronounced ah-gah'-pay) also means spiritual love or the love feast during communion.

I was agape when he said he was born with three nipples.

We were agog over the fact that our company is bringing in a full-time masseuse.

aggravate/agitate

We nitpickers are losing the fight to preserve *aggravate*. It means make worse or more severe. Traditionally, it is *not* a synonym for *annoy*. If you want to make me happy, you'll remember that people cannot be aggravated (use *annoyed* or *frustrated* or *irritated* instead). However, their injuries, diseases, and conditions can be aggravated. If you are *agitated*, you're shaken up and disturbed. You can agitate a person; that means you disturb them. To *agitate* also means to cause to move or shake, or to stir up attention.

Doing the Electric Slide aggravated my sprained ankle.

I think I agitated Maria; she's been banging her head against the wall for an hour.

agitate *see* aggravate

agnostic/atheist

Agnostics aren't sure whether there's a God or not. They believe that no one can possibly know until he or she dies. *Atheists* don't believe in God. Although it's usually associated with religious beliefs, *agnostic* can also mean skeptical or unwilling to express an opinion.

The agnostic proclaimed on her deathbed, "Well, I guess I'll find out soon."

Ike is such an atheist that he crosses out "In God We Trust" on all of his dollar bills.

ago/since
Ago and *since* should never be used next to each other, as in this sentence: "It was two years ago since her parents got divorced." Use one or the other, but not both. *Ago* refers to a time in the past, and *since* tells us what happened between that past time and now.

Ten years ago, my daughter was a flower girl, and now she's a bride.

It has been at least three days since you fed our goldfish.

agog *see* agape

ahoy
Did you ever wonder what a sailor means when he says "Ship ahoy"? "When someone says 'ship ahoy,' he means a ship is approaching or present," says fisherman Mark Glatzer. *Ahoy* can also be used as a greeting, like "hello." When the telephone was invented, people answered the phone "Ahoy, ahoy."

When the Coast Guard boat approached in the fog, the captain of the boat in distress called out, "Ahoy! The engine seized and we've run out of beer!"

akimbo

Akimbo means bowlike. Your arms are *akimbo* when they're bent, elbows outward, with your hands on your hips, so if you're standing *akimbo*, you're standing with your hands on your hips. According to some dictionaries, other things can be *akimbo*, too, if they're bent or in a bowlike position. *Akimbo* can function as an adverb or an adjective.

I stood akimbo as he related the story of where he had been until 3 A.M.

Peggy was akimbo while her child explained how the doll head got into the toilet "all by itself."

ale/lager

The distinction between these two terms has nothing to do with the color or bitterness of the beer. The difference is merely in what kind of yeast (*ale* yeast or *lager* yeast) is used in the brewing process. "With the exception of a very few beer styles that use unique bacterium, ale and lager are the only two types of beer," says brewmaster Marc Gottfried of the Morgan Street Brewery in Missouri. "All of these other words we hear, such as pilsner, stout, bock, and oktoberfest, are nothing more than the formal names of certain beer styles. All of these styles use either ale or lager yeast."

Marin Brewing Company's White Knuckle Ale took the bronze medal in the World Beer Cup 2002.

In college, people who drank the lager Miller Lite got teased relentlessly.

all together/altogether

All together means everyone (or everything) at once; as a group. *Altogether* means completely.

Sometimes people at traffic lights look at us strangely when they see my family singing Simon and Garfunkel songs all together at the top of our lungs.

It is altogether ridiculous to suggest that I should quit eating doughnuts just because I eat a dozen a day.

all-around/all-round

Don't bother checking your dictionary; it'll tell you these terms are synonyms. However, I believe *all-round* makes more sense. Just like *well-rounded*, *all-round* describes something that is complete, like a circle. *Around* describes things that surround a center, or are near.

Oswold is an all-round expert in air conditioning repair.

There are mosquitoes all around my tent.

alleged

Alleged is the victim of political correctness run amok. Everyone is alleged nowadays. We have alleged victims, alleged suspects; witness this ABC News headline: "Police shooting: alleged suspect in critical condition." Keeping in mind that the definition of *alleged* is "supposed, but without proof," let's tailor our word choices accordingly. If we know that someone was robbed, he is not the alleged victim; he's simply the victim. And if police have taken someone into custody, he is not an alleged suspect; he is a suspect. Period. You can prove that this person is a suspect by virtue of the fact that police have designated him so. What you perhaps cannot prove yet is whether or not he committed the crime; therefore, he is only an alleged criminal (until proven guilty).

The alleged bank robber wore a Santa Claus disguise.

allegory/fable/parable

Fables and *parables* are types of *allegory*. *Allegories* are stories in which the characters represent particular ideas or traits, such as a character that represents greed, or one that represents impatience. In *fables*, the moral is usually stated explicitly. Most fables are short, and many personify animals and objects or forces of nature. *Parables* also carry a moral lesson, oftentimes religious, but they generally rely on human characters rather than animals to carry their message.

Waiting for Godot *by Samuel Beckett is an allegory.*

Aesop is known as the master of fables.

Many stories in the Bible are parables, such as the story of the prodigal son.

alleviate

Alleviate means to make (a problem) temporarily less severe, without necessarily addressing the underlying cause. It is not a synonym for *remedy*. Be wary of any politician who talks about alleviating budget or health-care concerns.

The medicine alleviated my headache, but when it wore off, it felt like little elves with jackhammers were breaking up concrete on my brain.

alliteration/assonance

In case you've erased high school from your memory, *alliteration* is the literary device in which there is a repetition of initial sounds (usually consonants) in two or more words that are next to or close to each other in a sentence. Assonance is a repetition of vowel sounds, particularly in stressed syllables.

"Seven snakes slithered in succession" is an example of alliteration.

"One tub of fudge" is an example of assonance.

allot *see* **a lot**

all-round *see* **all-around**

allude/elude

Alluding to something is hinting at it, or mentioning it indirectly. If someone asks, "Did you get enough sleep last night?" she may be alluding to the opinion that you don't look good. *Elude* means to evade, defy, or baffle.

> *Are you alluding to the fact that I've gained a few pounds? (You louse!)*

> *Common sense continues to elude Bonnie, as she just asked if people in Australia drive "backwards."*

altercation

Altercation is not a polite word for a physical fight, no matter what high school deans tell parents. Rather, it is a heated argument that does *not* come to blows.

> *The boys got into an altercation about which one of them had eaten more Halloween candy.*

alternative/alternate

There are a few problems with *alternative*. The first is that, in Latin, *alter* means the other of two. Therefore, picky people will note that you should only have two alternatives, not many. Then there's the fact that it gets confused with *alternate*, which means to take turns or happen in succession. (The correct phrase is *alternating weeks*, not *alternative weeks*.) Finally, it's sometimes used when no choice is implied. *Alternative* means that you have a choice between two things; therefore, it's not appropriate to say you've found "alternative housing" for someone who has no choice between housing options.

My alternatives were to go to Boston or Seattle, and I chose to go to Boston because the bartenders are cuter there.

The author alternated between writing novels and writing dirty limericks.

altogether *see* **all together**

alumni
You are not "an alumni" of your school. *Alumni* is plural, and means *graduates*. The singular versions are among the rare nouns that are gender-specific in their spelling; a woman is an *alumna*, and a man is an *alumnus*.

During the reunion, the alumni got into a food fight.

ambiguous/equivocal/unequivocal
You'll hear the word *unequivocal* more often than *equivocal*. *Unequivocal* means clear and direct; *equivocal* means unclear and able to be interpreted at least two ways—usually done on purpose. That's why it differs from *ambiguous*: ambiguous also means unclear, but it doesn't carry the connotation of being

done on purpose unless you attach a qualifier, such as "intentionally ambiguous."

Lawrence sued the quiz show because he said the question he got wrong was ambiguously worded.

The politician's statements about raising taxes were equivocal; we were left wondering what his true stance was.

I'm not sure why you called her; I think she was being unequivocal when she said, "Even if hell freezes over, I never want to hear from you again."

ambivalence/apathy

Lots of people think *ambivalence* is synonymous with *apathy*, but it isn't. *Ambivalence* is the existence of mixed feelings toward someone or something, or a difficulty in reaching a decision. If you're *ambivalent* about something, you have opposing feelings about it, such as optimism and pessimism, love and hate, or happiness and sadness. If you're *apathetic*, frankly, my dear, you don't give a damn.

I had ambivalence about Betty's decision to transfer to another school; on one hand, I'd miss her, but on the other hand, I wouldn't mind comforting her boyfriend.

Your apathy about my new haircut is driving me bananas.

ambulatory

I know this sounds like someone is riding in an ambulance, but actually, it means related to walking, capable of walking, moving from place to place, or capable of being changed. Hospitals use this word a little differently, though. "A patient who chooses to use an ambulatory surgical unit is one who is usually in good health and not expected to need services that an inpatient in a hospital would require," says registered nurse Dawn Caceres. "In the medical arena we typically call these types of persons *outpatients*. Many facilities have sections called either the ambulatory surgery area or outpatient surgery area. The ambulatory surgery areas allow patients to efficiently receive short-stay minor procedural care. They typically go home the same day as surgery after being fully recovered. Recovery is usually done in a post-anesthesia care unit, many times just steps away from where the actual surgery is performed. Although, if the patient needs further monitoring, being admitted into the hospital for observation is available. There are other facilities that call this surgical area the 'Same Day Surgery' section."

My grandfather was not ambulatory after his tragic accident on my little brother's pogo stick.

ameliorate

If you want to be on the safe side, don't talk about *ameliorating* a problem. *Ameliorate* comes from the Latin word *melior*, meaning better. Ameliorating something means improving it, making it better. Ameliorating a problem would mean you're

am...

making it a better problem. Ditto for ameliorating pain; you're making "better pain." Instead, you might want to say that you're fixing or easing a problem.

To ameliorate the mood at the Department of Motor Vehicles, they hired a clown to distract people from the long lines.

amen

At the end of a prayer, do you know what you're saying when you say "Amen"? It means that you fully agree with the prayer. You're sanctioning it.

Please let this book sell a million copies. Amen.

among/between

Traditionally, you can only choose *between* two things. If you have more than two choices, then you're choosing *among* them.

Between intellectuals and blue-collar men, I prefer blue-collar men.

One day, I'll have to choose among my six boyfriends, but for now, I like them all.

amount/number

When you're talking about something that can be counted (even if there are too many to reasonably count), use *number*. For example, say, "There are a large number of dolls in her collection," rather than, "There is a large amount of dolls in her collection." Use *amount* when you're referring to something that can't be counted.

A small number of people showed up for the Apostrophe Preservation Society meeting.

A large amount of snow slid down the roof and buried the car that should have been in the garage.

ampersand
That's the sign that represents the word *and:* &.

If two screenwriters write a script together, their names are listed on the big screen with an ampersand between them.

anal
This word, all by itself, only means relating to or of the anus. It has nothing to do with neatness or an obsession with cleanliness or orderliness. If you want to insult someone properly, you'll have to say the whole phrase: *anal-retentive*. Sigmund Freud decided that children (aged 1½ to 3) go through an *anal stage* during which they get their pleasure from bowel movements and learn to toilet train. According to this theory, if parents are too hard on a child during toilet training, the child will experience anxiety about his bowel movements and will learn how to withhold his "junk." This child will grow up to be excessively neat and orderly, hence the phrase *anal-retentive*. The flip side of that coin is *anal-expulsive*, which is used to

describe someone whose parents were too lenient with toilet training and who grew up to be a careless slob.

I hope I never have to use an anal suppository.

My anal-retentive roommate follows after me with a Dust-buster when I eat my chocolate coconut doughnuts.

anarchism

"Although the word *anarchism* is understood by many in its classic sense (that defined by dictionaries and by anarchists of history), the word is often misused and misunderstood. Anarchism, because of the threat it imposes upon established authority, has been historically, and is still, misused by power holders [to mean] violence and chaos," says writer Jason Justice in his article "Defining Anarchism" (*www.anarchy.org/library/defanar.html*). Although anarchists are opposed to a structured government and capitalism, that doesn't mean they advocate aggression or bedlam. Most anarchists are opposed to all hierarchical institutions in which leaders have power over "followers." "All anarchists desire a society in which power flows from the mass of society upwards, not from the top downwards as is currently the case," says anarchist Darren Jones in his article "It's Not Easy Being a Watermelon" (*www.cat.org.au/aprop/itsnot.txt*).

Louis is an anarchist who thinks we could all get along without a government's intervention.

androgenous/androgynous/hermaphrodite

A *hermaphrodite* is a plant or animal having both male and female sex organs. *Androgynous/androgenous* can also be used to describe a person with both sex organs, or they can be used to describe someone who is not clearly male or female, someone or something with traits of both males and females, or something (like clothing) that is appropriate for both sexes. *Androgenous* means exhibiting a mostly feminine appearance. *Androgenous* also describes an egg that only contains paternal chromosomes.

The hermaphroditic oyster can fertilize itself.

She appeared much more androgynous after she cut her hair short.

The bank teller didn't know whether to call the androgenous young person "Mister" or "Ms.," so he just said, "Yo, you're overdrawn."

anecdote/antidote

An *anecdote* is a short story that's often told to illustrate an example of something. An *antidote* is a remedy that stops a poison from working. It can also be used figuratively to mean a cure.

Don't get my father started talking about fishing; he'll regale you with anecdotes about "the ones that got away" all night long.

Laughter is the antidote for sadness.

an

angel/angle

In the beginning of my relationship with my boyfriend, I was taking a picture of him, and I said, "I love the way you look at this angle." He replied, "I love you from all angles." It was the first time he'd said he loved me. Years later, I took out an ad in the newspaper on Valentine's Day. It was supposed to say "I love you from all angles." Imagine my horror when the newspaper arrived and the overzealous editor had "corrected" it to read, "I love you from all angels." Little did the editor know that he was editing an editor—an editor who knew darn well how to spell. These two words get mixed up so often, but it's usually the reverse; so many well-intentioned lovers write sappy poetry to their "angles." *Angels* are those winged creatures that may or may not reside in heaven. *Angles* are the shapes that occur when two lines meet.

An angel must have been watching out for me when I scored a hole in one and won the golf game.

Brush your teeth at a 45-degree angle.

angst

What a modern buzzword. Everybody has *angst*, particularly teens. And maybe because it's so often used to describe teens, people think *angst* means anger. ("So young. So angry. Damn that rap music!"—*Dr. Doolittle 2*) Well, guess what? *Angst* means anxiety, usually accompanied by sadness.

I'm experiencing angst about graduating from college: I'm nervous that I won't find a good job, and I'm sad to leave my friends behind.

annihilate/decimate

In Latin, the prefix *deci-* means one-tenth. Historically, to *decimate* meant to kill one in every ten men. Its meaning has been distorted over time, and now, most dictionaries accept "to destroy a large part of" as a definition, although careful writers may wish to find another word for this. Regardless of what you choose, it should never be used to mean "wipe out." The better word for that is *annihilate*, which means to eradicate, destroy, or kill off.

The child ran through my garden and decimated my strawberries; now I have fewer left to give away.

The hurricane annihilated my flower garden; I had to start planting from scratch.

annoy

If you're using a form of the verb "to be," then *annoy* takes the preposition *by*. If you're using a form of the verb "to feel," then annoy takes the preposition *with* or *at*.

I am annoyed by the man whose cellular phone keeps ringing in the movie theater.

Luke felt annoyed at the way Laura kept winking at another man.

annual/perennial/biennial

Let's talk gardening. An *annual* is a plant that grows for one year or season, a *perennial* lives for many years, and a *biennial* has a life cycle two years long.

> *Spinach is an annual.*
> *Trees are perennial.*
> *Some types of foxglove are biennial.*

anosmiac

We readily know the word for someone who can't see *(blind)* and someone who can't hear *(deaf)*, but what about someone who can't smell? The word for a lack of a sense of smell is *anosmia*, and a person who can't smell is an *anosmiac*.

> *Don't ask me if your perfume is too strong; I'm an anosmiac.*

anticipate/expect

Both words mean that you believe or think something will happen. *Anticipate* differs from *expect* in that an element of preparation is implied. When you expect something, you don't have to do anything to prepare for it. When you anticipate, however, you're getting ready for something. Be careful not to use *anticipate* if no preparation is required.

> *In anticipation of the children's arrival, I hid everything that was breakable.*
> *I expect there will be six more Austin Powers sequels.*

antidote *see* **anecdote**

antique/antiquated

An *antique* is something that was made long ago. *Antique* can also be used to mean old-fashioned, but if you want to be insulting, the better word is *antiquated*, which means outdated.

> *I bought an antique bee observation box on eBay for $500.*

> *Aunt Rita has an antiquated notion of courtship; she thinks any woman who calls a man to ask him out on a date is a hussy.*

anxious/eager

Think hard before you say you're *anxious* to see somebody. Are you really experiencing anxiety? Feeling *anxious* is not a good feeling, unless you particularly like being uneasy, nervous, and "on edge." The proper word for a positive sort of excitement is *eagerness*. A *New York Post* editorial says, "A lot of people in this administration have some old scores to settle, [Hillary Clinton] said in a TV interview last week, claiming that Bush is anxious to go to war." If that were the case, then Bush would not be ready for war; he'd be uneasy about it and probably using his pulpit to discourage us from entering into a war.

> *I'm anxious about my test results.*

> *I'm eager to see the look on his face when he sees I short-sheeted his bed.*

apathy *see* **ambivalence**

appears/seems

Appears is not synonymous with *seems*. *Appears* relates to a person's appearance. If a person *appears* sad, then he looks sad. Maybe he's frowning or crying. But he can't *appear* to be doing well in school, because there's nothing about his appearance that would indicate good grades. Yes, I know that some dictionaries accept *seems* as a definition for *appears*. Now ask me if I care.

Mrs. O'Henry appears excited about the new flavor of Girl Scout cookies.

The Thanksgiving turkey always seems as if it's moist while I'm roasting it, but my guests frequently ask for refills of their water glasses once dinner has been served.

apropos

For the record, let me state that I'm not a fan of this word. Most people toss it around as a more sophisticated way of saying "appropriate." It comes from the French *à propos*, which does not mean appropriate. Rather, roughly translated, it means "on the matter," and must be followed by *of (de)*. (Example: On the matter of baking cupcakes, who's going to volunteer?) On an Internet message board, someone wrote that a particular message was "very apropos for this list."

Actually, if *apropos* is going to take any preposition at all, it can only take *of*. As an adjective, *apropos* has come to mean timely and well-suited to the occasion. As an adverb, it can also mean "by the way."

Apropos, did you know Roger's middle name is Rufus?

Apropos of the last week of summer, we all went to the beach and tried to get tans that would last until the first day of school.

apt *see* **liable**

arbitrate/mediate
The role of an *arbitrator* is to listen to the cases of two parties who can't come to an agreement and then to make a judgment. A *mediator* doesn't have the power to make a decision; instead, his role is to help the two parties come to a mutually satisfying agreement.

I arbitrated between my feuding friends and decided that Moe should keep the lawn flamingo.

We couldn't stop arguing, so we asked Fred to mediate to help us decide how to split up the household chores.

arcane
I did an informal survey of a few friends, asking them to define *arcane*. All of them thought it had something to do with being old, like *archaic*. All of them were wrong. *Arcane* describes

ar...

something that's so mystifying that it's not accessible to the general public; it's only understood by a select few.

Our tax laws are dangerously close to being arcane; even some IRS workers can't explain some deductions.

aroma/odor

Aromas can only be pleasing. *Odors*, on the other hand, can be bad—and usually are.

The aroma of apple pie filled the kitchen, and I eagerly waited by the oven.

There is a foul odor coming from the baby's diaper. Check him for me, won't you?

artery/vein

An *artery* carries blood from the heart to other parts of the body. *Veins* carry the "dirty" blood back to the heart.

Coronary artery disease can lead to heart attacks.

I yelped when the student nurse took blood from a vein in my arm.

assassination/homicide/manslaughter/murder

Does it seem unfair to you that celebrities even get their own special word for *murder*? Well, guess what? *Assassination* does not just apply to public figures, as most people think. It actually refers to murder done in a secret or hidden manner. If a sniper is hiding in a tree and kills someone, that's assassination, whether the victim is famous or not. Of course, most well-known assassinations have happened to famous people, because it's hard for a murderer to get close to the intended victim. *Character assassination* refers to injury to a person's reputation. In legal terms, *manslaughter* applies to a person who has killed someone without the intent to do harm (e.g., a drunk driving accident), or as a "crime of passion" without premeditation. *Murder* is generally premeditated. *Homicide* is the catch-all term that simply means the killing of one human being by another.

President John F. Kennedy was assassinated on November 22, 1963.

The homicide rate in New York City has gone down.

The man who ran over a pedestrian was charged with manslaughter.

The man was charged with the murder of his wife.

assault/battery

Legally, *assault* doesn't have to be a physical act; it can be a threat or attempt to do bodily harm. If someone swings and misses, that's assault. *Battery* does have to be physical. Any unwanted touch is battery; it may or may not be a violent blow. In the southwest Florida *Sun Herald* article "What Is the Definition of Domestic Violence?" Bill Ropke writes, "Many years ago, when I attended the U.S. Navy's Officer Candidate School, the judge advocate general's course on military law explained assault and battery in the following manner: 'Assault is the communication of a threat and battery is the consummation, or the contemplation of the threat.' Therefore, if I was to say, 'I'm going to hurt you,' if the threat is perceived by you as being real, and if I was to just simply touch you, I have committed both assault and battery."

She committed assault when she threatened to kill him for coming home with lipstick on his collar.

A simple screaming match turned to battery when the drunken man began throwing punches at the baseball team's mascot.

assonance *see* **alliteration**

assume/presume
Both *assume* and *presume* mean to suppose something is true without having proof of it. I've argued until the cows came home and till rivers flowed upstream (well, almost) about the shades of difference between these two words. Some people think *presume* is the "stronger" word, meaning that it's more likely to be true. My conclusion: there isn't any darn difference. Let the grammarians turn blue trying to convince me otherwise. However, *presume* has extra meanings that assume does not: *presume* also means to do something without permission or to overstep your boundaries.

Just because I'm a woman, don't assume I know how to cook.
Halbert presumed to rifle through my garbage.

atemporal
The prefix *a-* means without, and in this sense, *temporal* means lasting for a limited period of time, so *atemporal* means timeless; independent of time.

Many people believe that our souls are atemporal; that they continue to exist even after our bodies die.

atheist *see* **agnostic**

auspicious
Having nothing to do with the word *suspicious, auspicious* describes a promising or positive future.

Earning straight As during the first term, the child was off to an auspicious start at school.

auteur
The French word for *author,* this is a word most screenwriters hate. It describes a film director (or, rarely, a producer) who exhibits creative control over a film, and usually gets a possessory credit ("A Film By"), even though he or she didn't write the screenplay.

Director Frank Capra is considered an auteur.

author/writer

Anyone who writes (published or unpublished) can call himself a *writer*. However, your work has to be published in book form to call yourself an *author*.

The male author of the romantic spoof Love's Reckless Rash *dressed up as a woman to promote his book.*

When the freelance writer saw her article published in a magazine, she was horrified: the title read "No Lime to Fear" instead of "No Time to Fear."

avalanche/landslide

An *avalanche* has occurred when a lot of snow or rocks come tumbling down from a mountain. When the avalanche pulls in other things with it, like people or trees, then it's called a *landslide*.

The Nature Channel showed footage from an avalanche, and the nearby town was covered with snow.

The hiker was almost killed in a landslide that sent pine trees flying through the air at him.

avenge/revenge

Both of these words mean to strike back against someone. However, *avenge* carries more respect. In the play *Hamlet*, Hamlet must avenge his father's death—meaning that he must retaliate in the interest of justice. If Hamlet was out for *revenge*, he would have been striking back just to make himself feel better.

Revenge is dirtier, and it doesn't necessarily have anything to do with fairness.

To avenge his son's humiliation, Elron's father spent the morning filing a complaint against the teacher.

Petunia slashed Yvonne's tires as revenge because Yvonne flirted with Petunia's ex-boyfriend.

average/mean/median

Let's say your bowling scores are 92, 95, 101, 105, and 125. To get the *average*, you add those scores together and divide by the total number of scores (five). Your average is 103.6. The *mean* is the number that's in the middle between your low score and your high score. In this case, your low score is 92 and your high score is 125. Add those two numbers and divide the sum by two to find the number in the middle, which is 108.5. To figure out the *median*, you determine which score is the "halfway" mark. In this case, there are five scores. There are an even number of scores lower and higher than 101, so 101 is your median.

I drink an average of five cups of coffee a day.

The mean age of people who attend our line-dancing classes is forty-five.

This week, Phyllis smoked a median of eighteen cigarettes a day.

averse *see* **adverse**

avocation/vocation

Many people think that your *vocation* is your job, and your *avocation* is your hobby. Alas, not quite. Proving how confusing English can be, your *avocation* may be either your main employment or your hobby. Further, *vocation* has the added possibility of meaning a calling, especially a religious one. After all, the Latin word *vocare* means to call or summon.

Her career is accounting, and her avocation is belly dancing.

Her avocation is accounting, and her hobby is belly dancing.

Melissa sees psychology as a vocation, not just a job, because she has known her entire life that she wanted to help troubled teens.

awakened/woken

"I'm sorry—I know *woken* is in the dictionary, but the word is *awakened*," says writer Linda Dewey. I agree! When you get up in the morning (or afternoon, if you're a sloth like me), you have *awakened*; you haven't "woken up."

I was awakened by the sound of shattering glass and a child saying "uh-oh."

awful

Awful comes from the Middle English *aweful*, and it originally meant full of awe. Nowadays, everybody knows the word to mean terrible, but "full of awe" is still its secondary definition. If you're

36 Words You **Thought** You Knew . . .

awful, you might either be lousy or inspired . . . confusing, no? (I can imagine the conversation now: "How are you?" "Awful." "That's great!") It can also mean massive, as in "an awful debt."

We were awful when we saw the street lit up by Christmas lights.

awhile/a while

The word *awhile* can only be used if you're referring to a short period of time. It's an adverb, not a noun, so if you're using the word *for*, you can't follow it with *awhile*. (Someone needs to tell that to the Ohio newspaper *The Plain Dealer*, which ran the headline "Aftermath of Strike to Linger for Awhile.") *Awhile* can only modify a verb, such as *rest* or *stop*. Most of the time, you need to use two words: *a while*, which can refer to any length of time—and can be preceded by the word *for*. Even famed humor columnist Dave Barry is not immune to this mistake: "Awhile back, I wrote a column . . ." Bad, bad Dave Barry.

Stay awhile and have a cup of coffee.

Stay for a while and try my wife's "meatloaf surprise."

Bb

bailiwick

A fun word, don't you think? It can be the district or office of a bailiff, or it can be a person's area of expertise or interest. Rarely will you hear someone say that something is in his or her *bailiwick;* most of the time, it appears in the negative form, like so:

Doing laundry is not in my bailiwick, so I usually drop it off to be done.

baited/bated

You do not wait with *baited* breath, unless you are hoping to catch fish with your breath. (You weirdo.) Indeed, you wait with *bated* breath, which means you're waiting eagerly or anxiously.

With bated breath, I wait to find out if I won the Elvira look-alike contest.

I baited my hook and hoped to catch a flounder.

bare/bear

"I once had a student write in a news story that someone who had been humiliated had to just 'grin and bare it,' which evokes a powerful image," says writing instructor Mary J. Schirmer. "However, of course, the student meant grin and *bear* it." *Bare* means to expose or to be naked (or lacking covering or decoration), or showing. It can also mean least possible, as in the "bare necessities." The verb "to bear" has about a gazillion meanings; among them, to carry, withstand, support, use, possess, yield, and to apply pressure.

When her groom insisted on wearing a Scottish kilt to their luau wedding, Princess Kameamea just had to grin and bear it.

battery *see* assault

because/since

People often use *since* as a synonym for *because*. It is not. *Since* refers to time: from a time in the past until the present (or a later time). "Since we have no apples, we can't make apple pie" is incorrect. The correct sentence would be "Because we have no apples, we can't make apple pie."

Since his divorce, Robert has been dating anyone with a pulse.

Because my cat is sitting on my keyboard, I can't type.

behoove

Behoove means to be necessary or appropriate. Most people erroneously use it to mean benefit, as in "It behooves you to do the extra credit work." Well, if it were necessary, it wouldn't be called "extra credit" work. Stick to the word *benefit* where it's needed, and save *behoove* for things that are imperative or proper.

It behooves us to change the baby's diaper.

bemuse

Next time you want to confuse somebody, you can *bemuse* him instead. It's a synonym for *bewilder,* and also means to occupy someone's thoughts.

Anthony bemused her with his technical computer talk.

benefactor/beneficent/beneficiary

A *benefactor* gives aid, usually financial. *Beneficent* is an adjective that describes someone who does good deeds and is helpful or charitable. Some dictionaries also accept it as a synonym for *beneficial.* A *beneficiary* is a person who receives a benefit, particularly money or goods from a will or insurance policy.

Our benefactor donated $1,000 to help us save the three-toed sloth.

The beneficent stranger offered us a ride to the repair shop when he saw our car was broken down.

We were the beneficiaries of his charity.

benign/malignant

There's only one word you want to hear when you've found a lump on your body: *benign*. That means it's not dangerous. *Benign* also means kindly. A *malignant* tumor is one that is cancerous. *Malignant* means life-threatening or wicked.

I'm a hypochondriac. Every time I get a pimple on my body, I have to go to the doctor to have him assure me it's benign.

The malignant creep liked to push elderly people in wheelchairs down flights of stairs.

bereft

Being *bereft* of something doesn't mean you simply lack it, but that it was taken from you, especially without your consent. If you never had something in the first place, you can't be bereft of it. The entertainment editor of the *Knoxville News-Sentinel* writes, "Justin Tosco's flat, quavering, thin voice confronts listeners right away on nearly every track, bereft of emotion and increasingly irritating with continued exposure." Oh, dear! Who stole Tosco's emotions? (Give them back!)

After the robbery, she was bereft of her Sony PlayStation.

berth/birth

Make sure you give someone a wide *berth*, not a wide *birth*, which wouldn't make much sense. To give someone or something a wide berth is to give space, literally or figuratively. As a noun, a *berth* is a ship's dock space, space for a ship to maneuver, a sleeping space, or a space for a vehicle to park. As a verb, it means to bring (a ship) into or tie up at a port.

Knowing that she had PMS, Jeff gave his girlfriend a wide berth.
Faye gave birth to the ugliest baby I've ever seen.

beside/besides

Beside means next to. *Besides* means in addition to or except. The sentence "Everyone beside Monica wanted to order pizza" means something different from "Everyone besides Monica wanted to order pizza." The former means that everyone sitting by Monica wanted pizza; the second means everyone except Monica wanted pizza.

I will stand beside you in good times and bad.
You're the greatest person in the world, besides me.

between *see* among

biceps

Surprise! *Biceps* is singular—identical to the plural form. So, even if you're pointing at just one flexed arm muscle, you have to say, "Look at my biceps."

Janie's left biceps is bigger than her right one.

biennial *see* annual

billabong

In case you're wondering where the clothing company got its name, *billabong* is an Australian word that signifies a usually dry streambed that fills only during the rainy season, a dead-end branch of a river, or a stagnant pool of water.

The billabong is a haven for insects.

billiards/pool

A *billiards* table has no pockets, as opposed to a *pool* table. In both games, you use a stick to hit a cue ball into other balls. There are several variations on both games. *Pool* is sometimes known as *pocket billiards.* Billiards may be played with three to twenty-one balls, in addition to the cue ball and object balls.

Billiards was once thought of as a "gentleman's game."
The pool hall is a popular hangout for teenagers.

birth *see* berth

biweekly/semiweekly

I want to have the last word on this subject. *Biweekly* is every other week, and *semiweekly* is twice a week. (And *bimonthly* is every other month, and *semimonthly* is twice a month . . . and so on.) There. Now the matter is settled. I can rest again.

We've decided to put out a biweekly newsletter for bald men and the women who love them.

The People Who Love Tattoo from Fantasy Island Club meets semiweekly, on Tuesdays and Fridays.

blatant/flagrant

Don't be too hard on yourself if you've confused these two. *Blatant* means offensively noisy, and by extension, it describes something done overtly and brazenly. It is more than a synonym for *obvious; blatant* suggests something negative, whereas *obvious* may be negative or positive. If a man is *blatantly* cheating on his wife, it's not only obvious, it's also offensively "in-your-face." The definition of *flagrant* is similar; it too describes bad behavior, but the emphasis is on the heinousness of the act rather than its overt nature.

When she gushed about how his tie matched the color of his eyes, she was blatantly kissing up to the new boss.

His flagrant disregard for others showed when he stole a homeless man's blanket.

blithe/blither

Blithe means happy and carefree, or showing a lack of proper attention. *Blither* means to talk foolishly; to babble.

She blithely left the house without a coat in the middle of the snowstorm.

I can't believe I listened to him blither on the phone for two hours about his brand-new bath mat.

boondoggle

This fun word can be a noun or verb and means a waste of time on an unnecessary activity, or to waste time or money on such an activity.

My husband said I was boondoggling when I color-coordinated his sock drawer.

bootless

I doubt you'd need a word for "lacking a boot" very often, so this word exists for an altogether different purpose: It means useless or futile.

After I organized the sock drawer, I took up the bootless process of cleaning his office. It'll be a mess again by tomorrow afternoon.

bow/stern and port/starboard

The *bow* is the front of a ship, and the *stern* is the back of the ship. If you're standing onboard facing the bow, the left side is the *port* side, and the right side is the *starboard* side.

In Titanic, *Rose nearly jumps off the stern of the ship.*

I stood at the bow of the ship to look for land, but all I saw were sharks.

We keep the life jackets in the cabin on the port side of the boat.

If you're going to get sick, please do so over the starboard side of the boat; we just cleaned the port side.

brackish

Brackish doesn't just describe mucky or muddy water; it describes water that is part salt water and part fresh water, and occurs naturally in places where a river meets the ocean (estuaries). Brackish water contains .5 to 30 grams of salt per liter.

Puffers should be kept in a brackish tank.

breech/breach

A *breech* is the part of a gun behind the barrel where bullets can be loaded. It also is the human buttocks (or the emergence of a newborn buttocks-first rather than head-first). A *breach* is an opening, gap, split, violation (as in a law or contract), or an alienation of a relationship. The correct phrases are as follows: breech birth, breach of contract, step into the breach, and a family breach.

If the baby is in a breech position, I'll probably need stronger drugs to get through the labor.

We don't speak to my father's side of the family because of a family breach that started when my uncle mooned my mother.

bring/take

You *bring* something toward you, and *take* it away from you. *Bring* means to carry something from a more distant place to a place nearer to the speaker, and *take* means the opposite:

to carry something from a place near the speaker to a farther place. You don't bring something to a party—you take it there.

Bring me the doughnuts—I'm starving!
Take these doughnuts into the other room before I eat all of them.

bromide

A *bromide* is a cliché: an overused expression like "clean as a whistle" or "white as snow." A person who is described as a *bromide* is sort of a walking cliché, someone who is unoriginal and not clever.

Your essay is so full of bromides that it sounds as if you have no thoughts of your own.

brutalize

The two definitions of this word are flip sides of a coin; *brutalize* can mean to treat someone cruelly (though not necessarily with physical violence—you can verbally or emotionally brutalize someone), or it can mean to make someone else *become* brutal because you've treated him or her harshly.

The lawyer tried to sway the jury to believe that the defendant had been brutalized by child abuse, but the jury thought that was a crock and convicted him anyway.

bulimia

It's a common misperception that all people with *bulimia* vomit after a meal. Bulimics binge and purge. A bulimic may purge in a variety of ways: by stopping eating altogether after binging, by obsessively exercising, taking laxatives, or by vomiting. If a person does not binge, but rather tries to starve herself, that's *anorexia*.

The young dancer had bulimia; she would eat and then take a laxative after every meal.

bunghole

Beavis and Butthead made viewers giggle at this "dirty word," which in fact, is in no way obscene. It's the hole in a keg, cask, or barrel for filling or emptying it. The company Bunghole Liquors even sells a T-shirt that says "Bunghole is not a dirty word."

We poured the beer out of the keg's bunghole.

burglary/robbery

It's *burglary* if it involves an illegal entry; burglars enter buildings uninvited and steal, or intend to do so. *Robbery* doesn't have to include a break-in; to be a robber, one simply has to steal something.

There was a burglary at the gas station last night; someone stole all the free matchbooks.

I noticed I had been robbed when I tried to pay for my doughnuts and found my wallet empty.

bust
Unless you're talking about a sculpture that shows a person from the chest up, or a person's chest, or causing something to go broke, or taming a horse, the word *bust* is slang. When you mean burst ("we bust open the piñata"), broken ("the machine is busted"), or caught ("he got busted for drug possession"), don't use *bust* in formal writing.

Linus in the Peanuts cartoons has a bust of Ludwig von Beethoven on his piano.

Cc

cacophony
Cacophonies are unpleasant. I've heard this word used to mean conglomeration, as in "There's a wide cacophony of food at the buffet." This is wrong. *Cacophony* can only be used to mean a mixture of sounds causing a harsh effect.

I could barely hear the boy band over the cacophony of screaming fans.

cadge
Cadge is only a verb, and it means to mooch or beg. The noun form is *cadger,* signifying a huckster.

She cadged a free T-shirt from the proprietor.

Caesar/C-section/Ceasar
Both the Roman Emperor Julius and the salad are spelled the same way: *Caesar* (not *Ceasar*). And *C-section,* short for *Caesarian section,* was named so because of the belief

that Julius Caesar was delivered by C-section (during which the baby is pulled out of an incision in the mother's abdomen and uterus). However, this story is not likely, as his mother would have almost certainly died during childbirth if this were the case; medical procedures weren't nearly as advanced then.

The waiter spilled my Caesar salad all over my lap.

I'm far too much of a wimp for labor, so I'm having a C-section.

calamity/calumny

A *calamity* is a devastation—a great loss because of misfortune. The noun *calumny*, however, is an untrue piece of gossip intended to harm a person's reputation or status, or the act of defamation.

The death of their son was a calamity for the Browns.

It turned out that the story about Jane's being a stripper was just calumny.

callous/callus

The hardened bump on your skin is a *callus*. Someone who is uncaring is *callous*.

After shoveling dirt all day, I got a callus on my hand.

The callous neighbor saw Iris struggling to carry her groceries, but he didn't offer to help.

callow

Yes, it sounds like *shallow* or *callous*, but actually, it means acting in an immature fashion or lacking in experience or sophistication.

Don't be so hard on him; he's just a callow teenager who doesn't understand why it's not okay to call the priest "dude."

calumny *see* **calamity**

camaraderie/comrade

The spelling on these can be tricky. Remember that *camaraderie* is not spelled "comraderie," even though the root words are related. *Camaraderie* is a feeling of closeness among or between people; a *comrade* is a friend or fellow group member.

After sharing the experience of camping together, the Girl Scouts enjoyed greater camaraderie.

I asked my comrade to come hold my hand while I had a blood test done.

can/may

Most of us know the difference between *can* and *may*, but we still slip up. "Can I go to the bathroom?" Well, yes, you probably have the ability to go to the bathroom. Whether or not you have permission is another story. Use *may* when you're asking for consent.

I don't know if I can stay awake during the entire movie Titanic.

May I date your daughter if I promise never to touch her below the chin?

canceled/traveled

Canceled and *canceling* only have one "l" per word, as do *traveled* and *traveling*.

I canceled the romantic getaway weekend because my girl-friend dumped me for her dentist.

I traveled that weekend anyway, and I met a great flight attendant.

canny

You've probably used the word *uncanny* (mysterious or inexplicable), but have you ever wondered what *canny* meant? Well, I hope you have, because I'm about to tell you: It means clever, acting in one's own best interest, thrifty, or (primarily British) pleasant. Quite a few applications for this word, and not one of them the opposite of *uncanny*!

She was canny when she made up the schedule; did you notice she's only hosting one meeting at her house but expecting the rest of us to host two?

capitulate

Capitulate means to surrender, to give in, or accept defeat.

> *Despite the fact that I had plans for Saturday, I capitulated to my sister's request for a babysitter.*

careen/career

Probably because *careen* is most often heard in the context of a car careening off a cliff, people think it means to plummet. Actually, it means to swerve from side to side. If a car just drives straight off a cliff, it hasn't careened. Similarly, the verb *career* means to speed (often used when describing cars).

> *The car careered through the red light and then careened down the hill before crashing into a pile of shopping carts.*

casualty

Don't know about you, but I always thought a *casualty* was a death. It's not necessarily so. Casualties include those who are injured or harmed, as well. *Casualty* can also refer to the accident itself.

> *The train wreck caused many casualties, but everyone was lucky enough to escape alive.*

catalyst

A writer wrote to me to say she was having trouble convincing her writing group that *catalyst* was not a religious word. I haven't the foggiest idea where they'd get such a notion, but I'm here to set the record straight: A catalyst is an agent of change—something or someone that sets off a process.

Seeing his wife gawk at the lifeguard was the catalyst that convinced him to start going to the gym.

caveat

A *caveat* is a warning. It's not an "extra note," an exception, or an explanation. When someone says "one caveat," she means there's one thing you need to watch out for. *Caveat emptor* means "buyer beware."

I'll sell you my car, but with a caveat: it doesn't run.

celibate

Did you know that you can have sexual intercourse and still be considered celibate? The original meaning of the word was simply "unmarried," although I admit that you'd be stretching it to call yourself *celibate* today using only that qualification.

She remained celibate until she met the love of her life.

census/consensus

A *census* is an official count of the population, and in the United States, there's one every ten years. I vote for *consensus*

as "Misspelled Word of the Year." Note that it's *consensus*, not "concensus." But beyond that, it's also a nominee for "Most appearances in a redundant phrase." A consensus is a generally accepted opinion. Therefore, a *consensus of opinion* or a *general consensus* is just restating the definition.

My cousin got a temporary job as a census-taker and hasn't worked a day since then. I'm looking forward to the next census so he can pay me back the money I loaned him.

We reached a consensus that it was time to order a pizza when we couldn't hear the television over the sound of our stomachs rumbling.

century/millennium
Each new *century* (100 years) and new *millennium* (1,000 years) starts with a year ending in 01. 2000 was not the beginning of the new millennium, as many people believed; 2001 was. Likewise, the next century begins January 1, 2101.

chattel
You may have seen this word in old books, especially in the context of a man treating a woman as a *chattel*. It means movable personal property.

Of all my chattels, I treasure my doughnut-maker the most.

chafe/chaff

As a transitive verb, to *chafe* is to make a skin irritation by rubbing, to warm by rubbing, or to bother. As an intransitive verb, it also means to become annoyed. To *chaff* is to tease in a friendly manner. (As a noun, it's also the covering of a seed—hence the expression "separating the wheat from the chaff.")

The bracelet chafed my wrist.

We chaffed him about his new mullet haircut.

chit

When I was in high school, one of my favorite teachers nearly got fired for swearing at a student. She wriggled her way out of it by claiming she had called him a little *chit*, a word that was originally used to describe an animal's babies, but evolved to an insulting word for a bratty girl. No one bothered to notice that the student in question was a boy. By the way, *chit* can also be used to mean a bill or note.

I told her to sit in the "time out" corner because she was acting like a chit.

choice/option

According to writer Steve MacKenzie, "If you need to decide between 'A' and 'B' you have two *options* but one *choice*." If you have several choices, then you must make several decisions; having two choices doesn't mean you're choosing between two things. It means you are choosing two things (out of more than two things).

I have to make a choice about which doughnut to eat first.

My brother says he's not married because he likes to keep his options open.

choose/chose

The present tense is *choose*, and the past tense is *chose*. *Choose* means to select or opt.

Karen threw her arms around the only man on the deserted island and exclaimed, "I choose you!"

Because he didn't know whether red or white wine went better with fish, Ollie chose to serve chocolate milk.

chord/cord

On your guitar, you strum a *chord*. If something hits home with you, it *strikes a chord*. You don't have any *chords* in your body, though: You have vocal *cords* and a spinal *cord*. And anything that's like a rope or a cable is a *cord*—like an extension cord.

Her impassioned plea for help really struck a chord with me.

I keep getting the telephone cord tangled.

chow/ciao

Chow is the slang for food; *ciao* (pronounced the same way as *chow*) is the Italian word that means hello or goodbye.

We're going out for chow. Ciao!

chronic *see* acute

circa
If you know the exact date, don't use *circa*. *Circa* is used when you're referring to an approximate date.

I started to lose my girlish figure circa 1985.

circumscribe/circumcise
One of the subscribers to my writers' newsletter, who shall remain nameless to protect her husband's job, writes, "My husband's boss always says 'circumcised' when he means 'circumscribed'!" You'd think that's something a man wouldn't confuse. In case you're not sure, *circumscribe* means to encircle, confine, or limit. *Circumcise* means to cut the foreskin off a penis, or to remove all or part of a clitoris.

I circumscribed my teenager's spending at the mall by taking back my credit card.

They chose to have the baby circumcised.

circumspect
I've heard this word used to describe someone who is worthy of suspicion—maybe because it sort of rhymes with *suspect*? Instead, this word should be used to describe someone who is cautious and wary of circumstances.

He was circumspect about revealing his personal infor-

mation to the person in the chat room who called herself "NeedsASugarDaddy47."

cite/site/sight

You *cite* facts, visit a Web *site*, and use your sense of *sight*. To *cite* is to point something out (especially to prove a point), to praise, or to officially name someone in court. You can visit a *site* (a place). *Sight* should be used as a noun, meaning the ability to see or something you are seeing. It shouldn't be used as a verb ("I sight a rare bird in the distance")—that's just pretentious. Use *see* instead, or if that's just too common for your taste, try *spot*.

> *He cited an American Psychological Association study to prove that anxiety disorders are on the rise.*

> *Is this the site where the Donny Osmond fan club will meet?*

> *I realized my sight wasn't as good as it used to be when I threw my arms around a complete stranger at the restaurant, thinking he was my husband.*

clairaudient/clairvoyant/ESP/medium/telepathic/telekinetic/psychic

Someone who is *clairvoyant* can "see" the future, or perceive things beyond the scope of humans' five senses. *Clairaudient* describes someone who can "hear" sounds that are not in the physical realm. *ESP* stands for "extrasensory perception" and encompasses any paranormal abilities that can't be explained in terms of our five senses. A *medium* is a person who passes messages back and forth between dead people and living people. Someone who is *telepathic* can read people's minds. If you can move things with the power of your mind, you're *tele-kinetic*. *Psychic* is a catch-all term that describes anyone whose mental abilities lie outside the range of science. Contrary to popular belief, you don't have to be able to predict the future to be psychic—you may know mysterious and inexplicable things about the past or present, instead.

classic/classical

Not only is the word *classic* misused, but it's overused. It's an adjective that is in danger of becoming meaningless if we keep throwing it around all willy-nilly. A week after they come out, all Disney movies are touted as *classics*. To truly qualify as a *classic*, something has to have withstood the test of time. Its value must still be as great today as it was when it was first published, produced, or invented. I completely reject the phrase *modern classic*—you can say something is destined to *become* a classic, but it can't be a classic until a decent amount of time has passed (I admit this is no exact science). When you're talking music, *classical* describes a specific time period: it's European music from the late eighteenth to early nine-teenth centuries, or modern music that reflects that style.

The Adventures of Huckleberry Finn *is a classic novel by Mark Twain.*

Symphonies by Bach and Beethoven are found in the classical section of the music store.

collide

Your car can't *collide* with a tree, or any other stationary object. A *collision* is a mutual act that only takes place when both people or both things are moving. (You wouldn't say the tree collided with your car, would you? Or maybe you would. "Honey, that tree was out of control!") I should probably send a copy of this book to the California newspaper *The Almanac*; they reported that a vehicle "collided with a telephone pole."

We collided when we both turned the corner without looking.

comedogenic

I imagine it would be a bad public relations move for a company to advertise its product as *comedogenic*—which means promoting acne. Rather, you'll see that many cosmetics companies tout their products as *noncomedogenic*, which means that they don't cause acne.

My foundation was comedogenic—now I have pimples all over my cheeks.

communicate

You're not *communicating* unless the other person understands you. You can't communicate at a person. If you try winking and smiling at someone, but he doesn't understand that you were flirting, then you have not achieved nonverbal communication. You've simply winked and smiled, probably to a really oblivious man.

We communicated about our hopes that Carrot Top's recent surge in popularity would die down quickly.

compendium/compilation

Both of these words can refer to a list or collection of items. However, a *compendium* can also refer to a summary or a short but complete treatment of a subject.

I didn't have time to read the whole book before the test, so I read a compendium of it.

She put together a compilation of love songs to give him on his birthday.

complaisant/complacent

Although both words can mean eager to please, only *complacent* means self-satisfied and contented to a fault. Personally, I think it's confusing to use *complacent* to mean anything *but* self-satisfied. If you talk about a complacent person, most people will assume that she's lackadaisical, even if you mean that she's eager to please.

She was so complaisant that she even offered to pick up his dry cleaning.

I'm afraid my workers have become complacent this week since they found out on Monday that I had already decided to give them all hefty holiday bonuses.

compleat

Not just a misspelling of *complete*, this somewhat archaic word is used to describe someone of particularly great talent, or an ideal representative of a group.

The compleat overachiever, she had already earned three degrees and won major industry awards by the time she was twenty-five.

complement/compliment

Complement is the verb to use if you mean "to highlight, set off, or perfect." As a noun, it means "something that completes or makes better." "You're pretty" is a *compliment*—a bit of praise or flattery.

That blouse complements your hair color.

I paid her a compliment for having completed her work so quickly.

compose/comprise

I've never met a word that can rile up writers quite like *comprise*. It is always wrong to say that something is "comprised of" something else. The word you want there is *composed*, and it's not interchangeable with *comprised*. Comprise means "to be made up of," so the *of* is already included. "Nobody seems to know that the whole comprises the parts, not the other way around," says writer Beth Kujawski. A quick trick is to substitute the word *contains*; if it makes sense, it's fine to use the word *comprises*.

My block comprises twenty houses.

The craft kit is composed of felt, glue, lace, glitter, pipe cleaners, and wiggly eyes.

compunction

Compunction is a feeling of shame or regret for one's actions or words, or a guilty conscience regarding something one is about to do. There is no verb form of *compunction*, although there is an adjective *(compunctious)* and an adverb *(compunctiously)*.

Lydia was suddenly overrun by compunction about cheating on her history exam and confessed to her shocked teacher that she had the dates of all the major battles written on her left hand.

comrade *see* **camaraderie**

concave/convex

*C*oncave is curved inward, like the interior of a sphere; *convex* is curved outward.

> *The poor pony's back was concave from being ridden so much.*
> *My mug handle is convex.*

concubine

Much to my dismay, I've learned that I am a *concubine*. The word has always meant *hussy* to me, but the truth is that a *concubine* is (a) any woman who lives with a man to whom she is not married, or (b) in certain cultures, a secondary wife. In case you're wondering, it's "a" that applies to me.

> *The concubine was getting impatient for a marriage proposal.*

concurrent/consecutive

If two or more things happen at the same time, then they happen *concurrently*. When things happen one after another, they happen *consecutively*.

> *The concert and the party are happening concurrently, so I can't go to both of them.*
>
> *I had three consecutive meetings in one afternoon, and all of them were equally pointless.*

confidant/confidante

This is one of those unusual nouns that has a male and a female form. If your trusted friend is a man, he's a *confidant*. If she's a woman, she's a *confidante*.

I told my confidante about my secret attraction to John Tesh.

confit

This is a culinary term that refers to something (usually pork, duck, or goose) that's cooked for a long time in its own fat, and cooled in its own fat to preserve it. This is a word that chefs often misuse: lemon confit or onion confit, for example, are impossible.

The chef prepared pork confit.

congenital/congenial

Congenital means existing from birth, and is usually used when describing medical conditions. A person who is *congenial* is friendly; a thing that is congenial is agreeable.

There are many support groups for adults with congenital heart disease.

My congenial friend strikes up conversations with everyone in line at the grocery store.

CO
.
.
.

congratulations

The proper spelling of the word has no "d" in it, unless you're trying to be cutesy and making a play on the word *graduation* . . . which I think is a groaner anyway.

Congratulations on saving thirty-five cents with your Preferred Customer Card.

connive

This word's true meaning was another surprise for me. When I was being manipulative to get my way, my mother would call me a *conniver,* so I always assumed it meant to be manipulative. *Connive* actually comes from a Latin word that means "to close the eyes." It means to close your eyes to a wrongdoing or something improper. To *connive at* something is to ignore it.

Juanita connived at her husband's drinking problem; she pretended not to notice that he came home drunk every night.

connotation/denotation

A word's *connotations* are the feelings or meanings suggested by that word that do not appear in its literal definition. Its *denotation* is its dictionary-style definition.

In my opinion, the phrase "New Age" connotes flakiness.

According to the dictionary, the denotation of bellybutton is "the place on the body where the umbilical cord was attached."

consecutive *see* concurrent

consensus *see* census

contagious/infectious

Dr. Preston B. Cannady, Jr., the program director for internal medicine residency at Finch University of Health Sciences / The Chicago Medical School, says, "Although both can mean the same thing, normally *infectious* refers to an agent causing the disease but *contagious* refers to the process or degree of ease of spread between people or other live animals. Malaria is an infectious disease, but it is not very contagious, as it takes mosquitoes or the spread of infected blood to another person to transmit the disease. Ebola virus is, however, very contagious via humans." Something that is *contagious* is capable of being transmitted by direct or indirect contact; something that is *infectious* can also be spread by other means.

Your bronchitis is contagious—stay the heck away from me.

Anthrax is infectious.

contemptuous/contemptible

If you're *contemptuous*, you feel contempt (or hatred). If you're *contemptible*, you're worthy of contempt.

He was contemptuous of his wife's gambling habit.

She thought it was contemptible that he used drugs in front of his children.

co

content/context

"I remember seeing golfer John Daly in a television interview many years ago, and he was complaining about being misquoted—that his words had been 'taken out of content,'" says writer Steve Circeo. Oops. Your words can only be taken out of *context*, not *content*. *Content* is the substance contained in something—the contents of your suitcase, the contents in an envelope, or the fat content of doughnuts, for example. It also refers to writing: The *content* of a book or article is what's written in it, and the *content* of a film is what was written in the screenplay. While I'm on my high horse, I'll take this moment to gag at a new term floating about: "content providers" as a title given to writers, particularly in the online world. Harrumph. Call me a writer, call me an author, a scribe, or even a hack, but never a content provider! *Context* is the environment in which something is said, written, or done that helps someone understand the words or action. When someone says, "Can you use that word in context?" he means he wants you to use it in a sentence that could explain how the word is used. If your words have been taken *out of context*, it usually means you've been made to look bad because someone has only quoted part of what you said without explaining the whole story.

The content of the novel was so moving that I had weeping spells at work when I read my book at lunch.

In the context of a fire station, the words "we have an emergency" mean something entirely different than they would in a preschool.

continual/continuous
Continual is on a regular basis, but with breaks in between times. *Continuous* has no breaks. You may continually get headaches, but if you have them continuously, then it means you never stop having a headache.

I continually get caught singing in my car at stoplights.

He worked continuously for twelve hours on his time travel machine.

convex *see* concave

convince/persuade
This one's probably a lost cause, but if you want to be very careful, you may want to note the distinction between *convince* and *persuade*. You can convince people *of* something or *that* something is right/wrong, and persuade people *to do* something. You can't convince someone to do something. *Convincing* deals with opinions, and *persuading* deals with actions. If all someone has done is changed your mind, then he or she has *convinced* you. If you've acted as a result of someone's suggestion, then he or she has *persuaded* you.

Amy convinced me that I should apologize to my ex-husband for filling his gas tank with marbles.

Of course, Amy's the one who persuaded me to buy the marbles in the first place.

coop/coup/coupe

Writer Melodee Heberden says, "I have a friend who thinks *coup* is the same as *coop*. She even will say a 'chicken koo,' thinking she's pronouncing it right. I've tried to tell her, but she doesn't believe me." Well, Melodee's friend, if you want to keep sounding silly, far be it from me to stop you. But if you want to get it right, a *coop* (with the "p" sound at the end!) is a cage for small animals. If you feel confined, you might say you feel *cooped up*. A *coup*, on the other hand, is a French word (pronounced with no "p" sound at the end) that means a surprising or exciting feat. A *coupe* is a two-door car.

How did the chickens get out of their coop?

Getting signed to a major record label was a coup for the band.

I bought a coupe to replace my SUV so my friends would quit using me as the group taxi driver.

copyrighted/copywriting

A piece of work that has been registered with the Library of Congress is *copyrighted*, not *copywritten*. *Copywriting* means writing advertising copy (the words that appear in advertisements and promotional material). By the way, copyright exists from the moment the work is fixed in a tangible medium of expression, whether or not you register the work.

I copyrighted my "Ode to the Person Who Invented Doughnuts."

I began my copywriting career by writing a brochure for a singing telegram company.

cord *see* chord

councilor/counselor
"A *counselor* is an attorney. A *councilor* is a member of a city council or some other council or law-making body," says writer LeAnn R. Ralph. Further, she adds that when you go to a lawyer, you're seeking legal *counsel*, not legal *council*. A *counselor* may also be someone who offers guidance or psychological help.

I'm seeing a counselor to help me overcome my fear of vegetables.

The councilor resigned after two years on the job.

coup *see* coop

couple/few/several
A *couple* is only two, never more. A *few* is any small number above two. *Several* is an unspecified small number that's more than two.

I only got a couple of hours of sleep last night.

I get cranky if I go more than a few days without a massage.

My cat has singed off her whiskers several times by sticking her face too close to a candle.

cracker/hacker

There's a growing group of computer whizzes who are getting irritable about the use of the word *hacker* to mean someone who tries to crack security codes, break into computer systems, and write viruses. According to this group, a *hacker* is anyone who is very knowledgeable about computers (programmers, for example), and the correct word for those other scumbags is *cracker*.

Walter is our resident hacker; he can fix any computer problem.

Leon is a pimply-faced cracker who spends his worthless and pathetic days devising ways to erase people's hard drives by sending electronic viruses in e-mail messages.

credible/credulous/incredulous

Credible means able to be believed. *Credulous* means gullible; believing whatever you are told. Its antonym is more frequently heard: *Incredulous* means skeptical, or not wanting to believe.

I found her story about her fiancé's illness to be credible because I saw her buying only chicken noodle soup at the supermarket.

I was credulous as a teenager; when my friend told me that you have to shave kiwis before you eat them, I believed him, and did so—until I heard my friends giggling in the background.

I am incredulous about the tabloid story that says Brad Pitt has an alien baby.

creed
Although *creed* can be used to describe religious beliefs, it doesn't have to be used that way. *Creed* can mean any set of beliefs or principles that govern the way you live. It is synonymous with *credo*.

My creed is "Success is worthless without someone to share it with."

criteria
Criteria is a plural noun. The singular form is *criterion*. You cannot say "the criteria is"; it's always "the criteria are."

What are the criteria for applying for this job?

crony
You usually hear the word *crony* used in a negative way—"that hoodlum and his cronies." It's actually a much more versatile word; it just means longtime friend.

If Eric wasn't my crony, I would have beheaded him for awakening me at 4 A.M. to pick him up at the bar.

cull
When I submitted a screenplay to a production company, they

informed me that they would *cull* the best entries and show them to the company's executives. Many writers were rather confused, since *culling* traditionally means weeding out rejects; removing those of inferior quality. However, many dictionaries now accept *cull* as a synonym for select. Nonetheless, I'd still avoid using this term to describe choosing the best of a group.

They culled the brochures that listed the wrong seminar dates and put them in the recycling bin.

curriculum vitae/résumé

A *curriculum vitae* (or *C.V.*) is similar to a *résumé* in that they are both lists of qualifications. *Curricula vitae* are preferred in European countries. According to the University of Cincinnati's College of Law Career Planning Center, a curriculum vitae "is a detailed listing that usually includes publications, presentations, professional activities, honors, and additional information . . . Vitae are usually more comprehensive documents than résumés. They are most often used for academic or research positions, whereas résumés are the preferred documents in business and industry. Vitae typically include more information than a résumé and are more like a career biography." While a résumé is generally only one or two pages, a curriculum vitae may run several pages.

The British publisher asked me for a curriculum vitae.

Do you think the boss will ever notice that I said on my résumé I had been the president of Hawaii?

Dd

damask

I first heard the word *damask* in a line in the play *Starmites*: "Milady's damask cheek is far more fair than she has dared to dream." I assumed it meant soft, but we all know what happens when we assume. The adjective *damask* refers to the color of the damask rose: a deep pink. It can also mean an intricately woven pattern, a fine table or bed linen, or a kind of steel—but I think it's safe to assume that none of those descriptions applied to Milady's cheek.

I bought damask bed linen to match my light pink wallpaper.

data

Data is a plural word—so you can't say "the data is"; you have to say "the data are." The singular form is *datum*.

The data show that random acts of kindness are on the rise.

day player *see* extra

deadhead

Deadheading doesn't mean wearing tie-dye and following the Grateful Dead around. It's a gardening term that means removing dead flowers from a plant to encourage new growth.

I deadheaded the roses today.

debacle

A *debacle* is more than a bad situation. It's a total failure or disaster. Don't say you've gotten into a debacle if what you really mean is that you're in a quandary or conundrum.

Our garage sale was a debacle; not one person showed up. Perhaps we should have announced more than just our old sneakers for sale.

decimate *see* annihilate

defamation/libel/slander

According to publishing attorney Daniel Steven (*www.publish lawyer.com*), *defamation* is written or spoken injury to the reputation of a living person or organization. Injury to reputation generally is considered to be exposure to hatred, contempt, ridicule, or financial loss. *Libel* is the written act of defamation; *slander* is the spoken act. "This distinction is important; libel often has greater legal consequences than slander. Whether libel or slander, the defamation must be published—

communicated to someone other than the subject of the defamation. Truth is an absolute defense to defamation: If what you say is true, it cannot be defamatory."

The tabloid committed libel when it published an article that said the actress had a drinking problem.

The secretary committed slander when she told the board of directors at their recent meeting that the new teacher was having an affair with the principal.

defuse/diffuse

To *defuse* is to remove a trigger, or make something less volatile. You can defuse a bomb or someone's anger. To *diffuse* is to spread around.

The actor stormed off the set, saying "I don't work with roosters!," but the director defused the crisis by keeping the roosters far away from him except during shooting.

The perfume diffused throughout the conference room, making all of us gag.

deign

Deign does not mean dare. It means "to condescend; to do something you consider to be beneath you."

The celebrity deigned to go shopping at a mall as part of her video diary for MTV, although she sighed and acted aloof the whole time.

demagogue

A *demagogue* is a leader who wins support by riling up people's emotions.

Anne is a demagogue who was elected as president of the Parent-Teacher Association because she played on parents' fears about violence in school.

demise

Demise doesn't mean decline. Literally, it means death. By extension, it can refer to the end of something—a company that goes out of business, an annual event that gets canceled, a friendship that dissolves, and so on.

The demise of our relationship came after I found out that he was more interested in wearing my lingerie than seeing me in it.

demolish

Why is it that whenever you see or hear the word *demolished*, it's preceded by an adverb like *totally* or *completely*? *Demolish* is good enough all by itself. It means to destroy or tear down. Incidentally, *destroy* has the same problem—it's usually seen around town with *completely* and *totally*, when those words are "completely and totally" unnecessary because they're already implied.

The elephant demolished the piano when he stepped on it.

denotation *see* **connotation**

dependant/dependent
The noun that means "someone who depends on someone else" can be spelled either *dependent* or *dependant*. The adjective, meaning reliant, can only be spelled *dependent*.
My three dependants eat me out of house and home.
I am dependent on coffee to get me through the morning.

depends
"It depends whether or not I have to work that day." What's wrong with that sentence? *Depends* always must be followed by *on* or *upon*. The correct sentence would be, "It depends on whether or not I have to work that day."
I might go; it depends on how much alcohol you give me.

deprecate
Because we so often hear about someone's self-deprecating sense of humor, it's easy to think *deprecate* means insult. Not quite. It means to disapprove of. The use of *deprecate* to mean insult is a modern addition; you may wish to substitute the word *belittle* instead.
I deprecate men highlighting their hair.

de...

depression

Those who are familiar with psychology often cringe when a person describes him or herself as being in a *depression* or *depressed*. To be clinically depressed, a person must meet several characteristics described in the *DSM-IV*, the tool used to diagnose mental disorders. The person must have at least five symptoms, including decreased interest in nearly all activities, abnormal sleep patterns, impaired motor activity, fatigue, or difficulty concentrating, among others, for two weeks or more. If you want to be clear, you might want to say you have "the blues," or are "feeling down" if you don't meet the criteria for depression.

Abby was in a depression for two years after her husband died.
Lola was feeling down after her goldfish died.

desert/dessert

The *desert* is that dry, hot place with cacti and lots of sand. If you *desert* somebody, you leave him by himself. *Dessert*, the food you eat after a meal, is so luscious that it gets an extra "s." How to remember this one? You always want two desserts, hence "s" appears twice. I don't know about you, but I'd rather not spend more than one day in the desert.

It figures that our car's air conditioning would break while we're in the middle of a desert.

What do you mean there's no dessert? I have been craving chocolate ice cream all day.

destination
The only real final destination for any of us is the grave. I'm sorry to be creepy, but there you have it. If you want to take the word *final* a little less literally, then it's redundant in the phrase *final destination* anyway. By definition, a *destination* is an ending point and not a "stop along the way."

Our destination is Miami.

diatribe
Originally, a *diatribe* was a Greek term for a discourse or study that wore away at time. It came to mean an invective or verbal attack in the 1800s. If you want to compromise with the past, use *diatribe* when you mean a lengthy attack (that "wears away at time").

The angry mother launched into a diatribe against her daughter's boyfriend for calling her "ma'am," when she thought she was too young for the term.

dichotomy
A separation into two opposing or contradictory parts is a *dichotomy*.

Because of the dichotomy between academic writing and informal writing, Bill writes one way for term papers and another way in his journal.

didactic

Didactic can be used as an innocent enough word, meaning instructive, often carrying a moral lesson. But in general, you don't want to be accused of being *didactic*. It's typically used in a derogatory manner to insult a person who tries to teach others in a preachy or overdone fashion.

I got so sick of her didactic speeches about the dangers of smoking that I lit up a cigarette in front of her.

dieing/dyeing/dying

You'll probably never have use for the word *dieing*, which means to use a specialized device (a *die*) to stamp or cut. *Dying* is what happens at the end of your life, and you are *dyeing* if you're adding dye to something—like your hair or your clothes. I always wondered whether I was *tie-dyeing* or *tie-dying* . . . now I know.

Yesterday, I was dieing sheet metal.
I'm afraid the hamster is dying.
At this time tomorrow, I'll be dyeing my hair purple.

diet

This is being really nitpicky, but a *diet* is whatever you eat and drink on a normal basis. If you're trying to lose weight, you should say you're going on a *weight-loss diet*, because everyone has a diet—even people who are trying to gain weight.

I'm going on a low-fat diet to try to lose weight so I can fit into my old cheerleading uniform.

diffuse *see* **defuse**

dilemma/quandary
If you have a *dilemma*, you're torn between two things. If you must choose among more than two things, then you have yourself a *quandary*.

Frank treats me well, but George is more handsome, so I have a romantic dilemma.

I'm in a quandary; I don't know if red, maroon, or brown lipstick would look better with this dress.

din
A *din* has to be loud. There are no quiet dins, so don't use this word to describe unobtrusive background noise. A *din* is an unpleasant jumble of noises.

I could barely hear you over the din at the bar.

disassemble/dissemble
To *disassemble* is to take apart; to *dissemble* is to hide facts and use "spin control."

She disassembled the car engine and then couldn't figure out how to put it back together.

The corporate executive dissembled to assuage share-holders' fears about the future of the company.

disassociate/dissociate
There's just no need for *disassociate*. Some people think that adding an extra syllable makes them sound smarter, but really, *dissociate* does the job just fine. It means to break off relations or see as separate.

When she moved to Texas, she hoped to dissociate herself from her reputation as a floozy, but rumors quickly flew anyway.

disburse/disperse
To *disburse* is to pay out. You don't want to get that confused with *disperse*, which means to scatter or dissipate.

Why is it that slot machines never want to disburse any money when I show up to gamble?

The crowd dispersed after the celebrity stopped signing autographs.

disc/disk
The words are synonyms. For reasons unbeknownst to me, the preferred spelling for CDs, CD-ROMs, and the "cushions" in your spine is *disc*, and the preferred spelling for floppy and hard drives is *disk*.

After he fell off a ladder, my father had a slipped disc.
I saved my limerick about Swiss cheese on a disk.

discomfit/discomfort

To *discomfit* is to make someone ill at ease, whereas *discomfort* is the state of being ill at ease, or something that causes mental or physical pain.

She discomfited me when she asked if I wanted a mint; was she implying that my breath is bad?

The doctor told me I might feel some "mild discomfort" during the procedure; what an understatement!

discreet/discrete

Discreet people purposely don't attract attention to themselves. *Discrete*, on the other hand, means separate or unconnected.

She was discreet about the fact that she was looking for a new job.

The company has three discrete divisions.

disease/syndrome

"The term *disease* can be seen as having two uses," says pediatrician Dr. Len Leshin. "The more traditional medical use of the word has meant 'an abnormality of health.' For instance, a person at risk of having breast cancer does not have the disease unless the actual cancer cells are present. In this definition, a person with Down syndrome may be seen as healthy if he/she doesn't have any of the associated diseases such as diabetes or hypothyroidism. The term *disease* has also come to mean, in a more popular sense, any disturbance of the body away from the normal. So, you'll see the listing 'Down syndrome' in the National Organization of Rare Disorders rare disease database. In this light, you can call Down syndrome a disease, but you would also have to call Turner syndrome, acne, and hay fever diseases as well.

"The term *syndrome* refers to a number of physical or metabolic signs and/or symptoms that are all due to a single underlying cause. The syndrome need not be part of a disease. When first described, often the cause is not known (AIDS, Kawasaki syndrome); when the cause is discovered, the name usually doesn't change."

disenfranchise/disfranchise

Just like *disassociate*, *disenfranchise* is a useless word. Trim the fat and use its shorter synonym: *disfranchise*. Generally referring to the right to vote, *disfranchise* (and *disenfranchise*) means to remove a person's or group of people's powers or abilities.

Forty-six states disfranchise prisoners who are serving a felony sentence.

disingenuous
When you tell little "white lies," you're being *disingenuous*, or less than truthful.

I think he was being disingenuous when he said he liked my new haircut because I later saw him pointing at me and laughing.

disinterested/uninterested
Impartial people are *disinterested*. They're not necessarily *uninterested;* one would hope that a disinterested judge is interested in listening to the case before him or her. You're disinterested if you have no personal bias or stake in an outcome.

As a disinterested party, I was able to give Joe objective feedback about his flirting techniques.

I'm uninterested in any diets that don't involve doughnuts.

disk *see* **disc**

disperse *see* **disburse**

dissemble *see* **disassemble**

dissociate *see* **disassociate**

distinctive/distinguished

Distinctive points out how different or novel something is; *distinguished* compliments its renown or excellence.

Patty came up with a distinctive solution to the traffic problem: now she rides to work on an electric scooter.

The brain surgeon got an award for being a distinguished alumnus.

done/finished

"I do have a pet peeve," says Lydia Ramsey, author of *Manners That Sell: Adding the Polish That Builds Profits*. "I think that when people have had enough to eat, they should say that they are *finished*, not *done*. The cake is *done*, and the person is *finished*." I'd even take that one step further. The person isn't finished—that would mean the person has come to an end. If you take that literally, the person's dead. So, if you'd like to be really careful, say you *have* finished. (You would say, "I have completed the project," not "I am completed.")

His jury duty stint is done.

My grandmother finished knitting me a pair of pajamas; I guess it's too late to tell her I don't wear pajamas with feet anymore.

dosage/dose

"A *dose* is a specific amount; *dosage* refers to a regimen and is usually indicated as amount per unit of time," says Jon Reischel, vice president and public relations director of Loren/Allan/Odioso.

I took a dose of motion sickness medicine after watching The Blair Witch Project.

The dosage is five milligrams twice a day.

dual/duel

Dual is the word that means made up of two parts, or shared by two (as in *dual custody*), and a *duel* is an official fight.

This trip serves a dual purpose: to help me relax and to let me get a killer tan in time for my class reunion.

He challenged the man to a duel for ownership of the Mark McGwire home-run baseball.

dwarf/midget

According to the *Miller-Keane Medical Dictionary* (2000), "A *dwarf* in adulthood may be as small as 2½ feet tall. The proportions of body to head and limbs may be normal or abnormal. The dwarf may also be deformed, and may suffer from mental retardation, depending on the cause of the condition." The word *midget* is falling out of favor, but it refers to a type of dwarf; a person who is unusually small but average-proportioned. The word has been around since the mid-1800s, and was used as a label for proportionate dwarves in "freak shows." You can imagine, then, why many dwarves would rather see the word *midget* disappear. Many dwarf advocacy groups prefer the terms *little person* or *person of short stature*.

The dwarf was really sick of people asking if he liked The Wizard of Oz.

Ann Marie is a little person who married a basketball player.

dyeing *or* dying *see* dieing

dyslexia
This common learning disability is often misunderstood. A person who is *dyslexic* usually does *not* see or read words backwards. According to the International Dyslexia Association, dyslexia is a "specific language-based disorder of constitutional origin characterized by difficulties in single word decoding, usually reflecting insufficient phonological processing abilities." Simpler? A person with dyslexia can recognize letters but has trouble interpreting written language.

Although my dyslexic sister can name all the letters in her vegetable soup, she is unable to read the newspaper.

Ee

ESP *see* **clairvoyant**

each
Each is singular, so it has to take a singular verb, even if the noun it refers to is plural. For example, the sentence "Each of the dogs have a different favorite toy" is wrong, and must be rewritten as "Each of the dogs has a different favorite toy." Pretend that the word *each* stands for *one,* and you'll always get it right.

Each of the hospital patients gets two options for breakfast, and both options are equally disgusting.

eager *see* **anxious**

eclectic
Here's another one I didn't know until I started writing this book. I always thought *eclectic* was just another word for unusual. In fact, *eclectic* means chosen from a variety of disparate things; a

combination of different elements. If you have eclectic taste in movies, it doesn't just mean you like offbeat films; it means you have very varied taste and enjoy many genres.

Kevin likes an eclectic mix of foods. He dines at various restaurants that specialize in dishes from Thailand, Morocco, Russia, and Ethiopia, to name a few.

economic/economical
Economic isn't a word for thrifty—that's *economical*. *Economic* just refers to money and wealth; it doesn't judge how much money is involved. (Your car is not *economic*, though it may be *economical*.) Your *economic resources* are how much money you have. If you're being *economical*, you're being careful with your money.

The country is in an economic crisis because it can't pay its debts to the United Nations.

She has an economical lifestyle, preferring to buy things only when they're on sale.

eek/eke
Eek! Is it true that you don't know the difference between *eek* and *eke*? *Eek* is the expression of surprise or horror. To *eke out* is to barely manage to attain through exertion.

I eked out a living by writing bumper-sticker slogans to supplement my book royalties.

Eek! There's a mouse in the house!

effect *see* **affect**

effeminate/feminine
When you're talking about a man who has womanly qualities, instead of using the word feminine, use *effeminate*, because it was built specifically for this purpose. *Feminine* means characteristic of or relating to women.

His long hair and frequent manicures make him seem effeminate.

I like male singers, too, but I prefer feminine voices.

effete
Effete is not short for *effeminate*. If you're *effete*, you're worn out. *Effete* can also mean self-serving or decadent.

After spending all day chasing around two toddlers, I was effete.

ego/id/superego
Sigmund Freud thought that personality was divisible into three parts: the ego, the id, and the superego. The *ego* is the personality we present to the world, the *id* is hedonistic and is governed by biological urges (more sex, please!), and the *superego* is the conscience and "ego-ideal"—the idealized perception of the self.

He seems governed by his id; he's always eating or sleeping.

She has a submissive ego.
I could never shoplift—my superego wouldn't allow it.

egregious
If you've made a mistake that's truly awful and obvious, then it's *egregious*. This word's meaning has changed over the years; it used to mean outstanding in a good way.

I made an egregious error when I called the androgynous woman "mister."

either/neither
Both *either* and *neither* are singular nouns, so they take singular verbs. It doesn't matter whether the noun they refer to is singular or plural. ("Neither of the beds have been made" is wrong—the correct form is "Neither of the beds has been made.")

Either of the deodorants is preferable to no deodorant at all.
Neither of them would ever go out with the man in the Speedo.

eke *see* eek

elder/older
As an adjective, *elder* doesn't mean old. It means older . . . which can be very young. If you're eight years old, then your elder sister may be ten. Further, *elder* carries an air of respect that *older* just doesn't have.

I was taught to always respect my elders, which meant that I would never tell Grandma that I hated her cooking.

Although Ollie is only five minutes older than his twin, Wally, Ollie insists he went through puberty first.

electrocute/shock

Trust me—you've never been *electrocuted*. How do I know? Because if you had been, then you'd be dead. And you aren't . . . right? So what you've been is *shocked*. *Electrocuted* means killed by electricity, so *electrocuted to death* is redundant.

The judge ordered the serial killer to be electrocuted.

I got a shock when I touched the doorknob after sliding across the floor in my socks.

elicit/illicit

Elicit means to obtain or coax out; *illicit* means illegal.

I couldn't elicit a response from her on whether or not her coworker liked me, even after two glasses of wine.

She smuggled illicit goods into the country.

elude/evade

These words are very similar: they both mean to be difficult to pin down, obtain, or to get away from, but there's something shifty about *evade*. You can be *elusive* without being purposely sneaky or doing anything wrong. If you're being *evasive*, however, you're most likely up to no good.

I play the same lottery numbers every week in search of the elusive big win.

He evaded my question when I asked whose phone number was in his wallet.

e-mail
There may well come a time when it's standard to write *email*, but for now, *e-mail* (short for *electronic mail*) needs a hyphen.

I check my e-mail approximately every 8.6 seconds.

emigrate/immigrate
A person *emigrates* away from a country or region and *immigrates* to a new country or region. And, yes, a person who leaves his country is an *emigrant* of that country, just like a person who moves to a new country is an *immigrant* of the new country.

She emigrated from France to the United States.
She immigrated to the United States from France.

eminent/imminent
Eminent is an adjective of respect; use it when you want to point out that something or someone is praiseworthy, worthy of attention, or renowned. When something is *imminent*, it's about to happen.

Students spoke fondly of the eminent professor who always gave humorous and informative lectures.

You are in imminent danger of failing the cooking class because you have concocted only inedible food.

empathize/sympathize

You can *sympathize* with someone without *empathizing* with him or her. *Sympathize* has two definitions: to feel bad for someone and express your caring, and to be in agreement. *Empathize* means that you put yourself in another person's shoes—you identify with her and share her pain or trouble.

I sympathize with the boy whose mother gave him a perm.

I can empathize with Joan's desire to give up doughnuts, as I once tried to but struggled to last a week.

enervate

Writer Susan Stephenson says, "People use *enervate* similarly to *energize*, yet it means to lack vigor and energy." As a verb, it can also mean "to weaken."

Superman is enervated by kryptonite and can easily be overcome when in proximity to it.

enormity

Believe it or not, this one's not a synonym for *enormousness*. It has nothing to do with size; instead, it means heinousness or evilness. But that didn't stop *Dateline NBC* from reporting about the "enormity" of a boy's potential.

He was sentenced to life in jail because of the enormity of his crime.

ensure/insure

If you want to make certain, you want to *ensure*. If you want to take out an insurance policy, you want to *insure*.

Oliver ensured that his wife cooked him enough reheatable food to last him all six days that she would be out of town.

My home is insured against theft.

enthuse

Just take this word right out of your vocabulary. Tear it out of this book. Forget its existence, and mock people who use it. *Enthuse*, which some people use as the verb form of enthusiasm, was never meant to be a verb. Although it may be slightly more wordy, stick to "she was enthusiastic about the party" rather than "she enthused about the party."

envelop/envelope

To *envelop* is to wrap around, cover, or enclose. An *envelope* is the thing you put a letter in. (Duh. I know you knew that one.)

The house was enveloped in flames.

I got a paper cut on my tongue when I licked the envelope.

ephemera

Ephemera refers to things that are only meant to last, be significant, or have value for a short period of time. The singular form (rarely heard) is *ephemeron*.

I collect campaign buttons and other political ephemera.

epiphany

"*Epiphany* has really gotten out of hand," says writer Lawrence Benedict. "So many people are using it that I seem to be the only one around here who hasn't experienced 'the manifestation of a supernatural being' lately. Even the big Oxford lists that definition only (other than the Christian use). Christian faiths adopted *epiphany* to refer, specifically, to the presentation of Jesus to the Magi and, in general, to the various manifestations of Christ to the disciples, throughout the New Testament. Even though I now consider my religious thinking to be pretty eclectic, I was raised in the Church of England (in Canada) and have a particular nostalgia for 'Epiphany Sunday.' The current usage of *epiphany* seems to have drifted to something meaning 'a sudden enlightenment' or even worse, an 'Aha!'"

Mrs. Tanner claims to have had an out-of-body experience that included an epiphany.

ep
:::

epitaph/epithet

Don't get these two confused! An *epitaph* (not *epitath*, as it's sometimes misspelled and mispronounced) is the writing on a gravestone, or a short tribute about a deceased person. An *epithet* is a description or trademark that's sometimes used in place of a person's name, or an abusive comment.

I want my epitaph to read, "A nice person who knew the difference between 'your' and 'you're.'"

CNBC *market reporter Maria Bartiromo's epithet is "The Money Honey."*

epitome

I've often heard the word *epitome* used to describe something that's quintessential, or the ideal example—The Fonz as the epitome of cool, for example. Actually, *epitome* just means any typical example or representative, not the "perfect" one.

Mark is the epitome of a love-struck teenager.

eponymous

A person or group is *eponymous* if they've had something (a book, a movie, an album, an invention, a disease, a street, a flower, a building, and so forth) named after them.

Erin Brockovich is the eponymous legal assistant who inspired the movie.

equivocal *see* **ambiguous**

erstwhile

"I was guilty of using *erstwhile* to mean eager or earnest," says writer Mary Case. Oh yeah? Well, I was guilty of using it to mean "meanwhile." What it really means is from an earlier time; previous.

My erstwhile hairdresser gave me a bad dye job; that's why I'm coming to you.

esoteric/exoteric

If something is *esoteric*, it only holds appeal for or is only meant to be comprehended by a select few people. It can also be used to mean private. I never knew this word had an antonym, but it does: *exoteric* means it's for public consumption.

Lila made up an esoteric language that she uses with her best friend so her little sister can't understand that they're talking about boys.

Is this a confidential memo or is it exoteric?

euphemism

A *euphemism* is a more polite way of saying something that could be taken offensively or in a negative light—such as calling a car "pre-owned" rather than "used."

"Vertically challenged" is a euphemism for "short."

evade *see* **elude**

exalt/exult

To *exalt* is to promote to a higher status or position, to venerate, to glorify, or to hold in high esteem. When you *exult*, you rejoice.

We exalted the stage manager to the position of director after our last director came down with chickenpox.

We exulted over our large holiday bonuses.

except *see* **accept**

exoteric *see* **esoteric**

expand/expound

An interior designer on NBC's *Famous Homes & Hideaways* recently said, "You had a great idea for a color scheme that we just *expounded* upon." I guess she thought *expounded* sounded fancier than *expanded*. *Expound* means to make clear by going into great detail. And, no, the interior designer wasn't explaining her client's idea for a color scheme in great detail. What she was doing was *expanding* upon the colors that her client had chosen; adding to them. To *expand* means to make larger, or spread out. It can also be used similarly to *expound:* It can mean to go into detail (as in, "The governor expanded on his comments about the fire").

The speaker expounded on her method for paying off a mortgage in just five years, going into great detail about our payment plan until we started to fall asleep.

I'd like to expand our line of cooking products to include more microwavable items.

expect *see* **anticipate**

expedite
Starnet Design and Litho, Inc. advertises, "We are now able to offer our clients a tool to simply and quickly expedite these tasks." Well, that's redundant. To *expedite* is to speed up, so there's no need for the adverb *quickly*.

The grocery store hired more cashiers to expedite service to its customers.

exponential
You learned what an *exponent* was in math class. It's when a number is multiplied by a factor of itself. So why do we hear about "exponential growth" that's supposed to just mean large growth? That's not what it means. If something grows exponentially, then it is multiplied by itself at least once. So, if you want your $500 to grow exponentially, it must grow to at least $250,000.

X^5 is an exponential expression.

expound *see* **expand**

extant/extinct

Anything that's still in existence (not destroyed or extinct) is *extant*. If it's no longer in existence, it's *extinct*. And *extinct* isn't just for animals; a fire that's been extinguished is extinct, an inactive volcano is extinct, and other things that no longer exist (like slavery in America) can also be called *extinct*.

We know that Grandpa's World War II letters were still extant last time we checked the attic.

We were once best friends, but ever since Harry put a frog in my locker in the sixth grade, our friendship has been extinct.

extemporaneous/impromptu

Let's say you have to give a speech. If you do it *extemporaneously*, you're working without notes, though you may have practiced. If you do it *impromptu*, you haven't rehearsed or prepared at all.

Although he had practiced in front of a mirror, the self-help guru gave an extemporaneous speech about how to give speeches without practicing.

I had no idea they were going to ask me to speak about the mating habits of emus, so I had to give an impromptu talk, basing all my discussion on a nature show I vaguely remembered seeing several years ago.

extol

Don't *extol* anyone's praises. Know why? Because it's redundant. To *extol* is to praise.

I extol your patience with the little girl who keeps kicking your seat on the plane.

extra/principal performer/walk-on/day player

The Screen Actors Guild (SAG) balks at the term *extra* to signify a nonspeaking acting role, considering the word to be a pejorative. They prefer the term "background actor," with one exception: "Commercial nonspeakers are still called *extras* because of contractual language that enables a nonspeaker to be upgraded to *principal performer* if the actor meets one of three elements, one of which is to be in the foreground of the scene," says Gavin Troster, executive administrator of production services, SAG. "It was decided that it would be confusing to have 'background foreground' or 'foreground background,' so just call them *extras*. Confused yet?" A background actor or extra may also be called a *walk-on*. If an actor has lines—even just one or two—he or she is called a *principal performer*. A small but essential speaking part can also be called a *bit part*. A *day player* is a principal performer who is hired on a day-to-day basis rather than a longer contract.

The publicist warned the background actor not to make eye contact with the egotistical principal performer.

The Chewlie's Gum Guy in Clerks *had a bit part.*

I can't believe he got a standing ovation—he only had a walk-on role!

The day player on the soap opera prayed that her character wouldn't lapse into a coma or get murdered by a vengeful ghost before the season ended.

exult *see* **exalt**

Ff

fable *see* allegory

factoid
A *factoid* isn't just a short fact. It's an untruth that's been passed off as a fact, especially in the media, leading many people to believe it's true.

Aretha Franklin claims that it's a factoid that her mother abandoned her; the story was widely reported after Time *magazine quoted her as saying so.*

fag
Fag is the British slang for cigarette . . . causing many bewildered stares among visiting Americans.

Do you have an extra fag? I quit smoking last week, but I just can't resist any longer.

fantastic

The use of *fantastic* to mean "wonderful" is so ingrained in our language that I'm not sure how much impact I can have here, but I'm no quitter when the going gets tough. *Fantastic* means that something is based on fantasy; it's not factual. I'm willing to stretch the definition to include "strange" or "outlandish," but that's as far as I'm going!

I thought it was fantastic that my child saw ghosts in his bedroom; everyone knows ghosts don't exist.

farther/further

If you're talking about physical distance, use *farther*. *Further* is the word to use when you mean *more*, and aren't referring to physical distance.

This old Yugo can't go much farther.

Please think further before you agree to buy your six-year-old the Austin Powers in Goldmember *video.*

fax

One of my writer friends frequently e-mails me to ask me to "FAX" things to him. I always feel like he's shouting at me. Why, oh why, does this friend capitalize *fax*? The world may never know. It's not an acronym or even a proper noun. It's short for facsimile. Keep it lowercase. Oh, and it's also not a verb (you wouldn't ask, "Would you facsimile that to me?") . . .

but if I tried to enforce that one, the masses would probably throw pies in my face.

I visit the deli so often that they now send me a daily fax with their specials.

feckless/gormless
If you say *feckless* with a Scottish accent, it sounds really dirty. But it's such an innocent word! It means purposeless, pointless, or irresponsible. *Gormless*, a British word, means stupid or dimwitted.

The feckless young man missed work again today.

You must think I'm gormless if you expect me to believe he missed work because his grandmother died again. According to him, she died twice last month.

feminine *see* **effeminate**

feudal
"This word frequently appears in political writings and is now used increasingly as a synonym for unjust, tyrannous, or any other pejorative adjective for which the speaker cannot find the exact word he seeks," says *Baronage* editor Frederick Hogarth. "Correctly used it refers to a system of reciprocal loyalties between, in its original form, a landowner and its tenant, which requires the former to protect the latter, and the latter

to aid the former when called upon to do so. The chain of feudal relationships stretched from the prince to the lord to the tenant to the subtenant to the serf, with justice, political direction, and protection extending downwards, and counsel, labor, and military support extending upwards."

During the Middle Ages, the feudal relationship between lord and serf meant that the peasant would work the lord's land in return for protection.

fever/temperature

When Mom asks, "Do you have a temperature?" your answer should always be, "Yes." Everyone has a *temperature*, whether sick or well. The normal human temperature is 98.6 degrees Fahrenheit. Not everyone has a *fever*, however. Mom needs to revise her statement—either she needs to ask "Do you have a high temperature?" or "Do you have a fever?"

If you have a fever, did you really need to hug me?

My temperature is normal, but I feel like an elephant is standing on my head.

few *see* couple

fewer/less

For countable quantities, use *fewer*. You might have fewer apples or sick days. For things that can't be counted, use *less:*

less water or sunshine. The one that confuses people most is money: No, it can't be counted. You can count dollars and cents, but there's no such thing as one money, two moneys, etc. So it's okay to say "less money."

There were fewer angry people at the "returns" desk today, so the customer service person was less crabby than she was yesterday.

fiction/nonfiction

Fiction is made up by its author; it's not a true account. Novels are fictitious. *Nonfiction* (which doesn't need a hyphen, by the way) is true. Biographies and newspaper articles are nonfiction. There is a third category called *creative nonfiction,* and that encompasses true stories that are told in a creative or literary way, such as personal essays and memoirs. In other words, they're not told in a dry "timeline" fashion.

Carrie *is a work of fiction by Stephen King.*

I wrote a nonfiction book about how to raise chinchillas for fun and profit.

figuratively/literally

How many times have you heard a person say something like, "I was literally jumping out of my skin"? I hope it makes you cringe as much as it does so to me. *Literally* means it's the exact truth, to be taken at face value. I've never heard of someone actually jumping out of his skin, so I'm going to surmise that these people mean to say *figuratively*. *Figurative* means *not* literal but rather a figure of speech or metaphor.

Sue Ellen figuratively pulled out her hair when her seven-year-old asked her, "Mommy, where do babies come from?"

My hairdresser literally cut off six inches of my hair when I asked for a "trim."

finished *see* **done**

firstly

Now here's a stupid word if ever there was one. There may be no other word that screams "I'm trying to sound more intelligent by adding an extra syllable" louder than *firstly*. My first piece of advice is: Don't use this word. My second piece of advice is: If you simply must, then you have to follow it up with *secondly*, *thirdly*, and so on. You can't say "firstly" and then follow it with "second" and "third." The reverse is also true: You can't say "first" and follow it with "secondly."

Firstly, spin around three times. Secondly, try to pin the tail on the donkey.

First, try to forget that you ever saw the previous example. Second, try to remember this one.

flagrant *see* **blatant**

flammable/inflammable

I know this one is weird, but these words are synonyms. They both mean that something is able to catch on fire. Considering that, you might as well go with the shorter word.

I found out that my pants were flammable when I flicked my lighter in my pocket and soon found myself stopping, dropping, and rolling.

flaunt/flout

When you *flaunt* something, you make a grand display of it or show it off. You don't flaunt authority. You *flout* it. Well, if you're an authority-flouting kind of person, that is. *Flout* means to scorn or refuse to comply with.

He flaunted his good looks by having pictures of himself all over his house.

She flouted her curfew by staying out all night.

flier/flyer

Every time I wanted to print up a paper to hand out, I wasn't sure if I was printing up a *flier* or a *flyer*. Turns out that it doesn't matter. Either spelling is acceptable for both meanings (those having to do with flying and papers for circulation). Preferably, handouts are spelled *flyers* and someone who flies is a *flier*.

The nightclub worker passed out flyers to promote their annual Elvis karaoke contest.

Because I'm addicted to getting "frequent flier miles," I paid my college tuition by credit card.

flotsam and jetsam

Flotsam and *jetsam*, rarely seen apart, are used to mean assorted junk. But just in case you're wondering what each word means, *flotsam* is the junk that floats out to sea after a shipwreck, and *jetsam* is the stuff that's been thrown overboard and washes ashore or sinks.

Our attic houses all sorts of flotsam and jetsam that we can't bring ourselves to throw out.

flout *see* flaunt

flummox

Someone *flummoxes* you when they bewilder you. *Flummoxed* means confused.

I didn't mean to flummox you with my directions. I'm sorry you ended up in the wrong state.

flyer *see* flier

folderol

"Picture, if you will, a medieval minstrel singing a ballad," say Mike and Melanie Crowley, founders of *Take Our Word for It*, a word origin Webzine (*www.takeourword.com*). "He is making it up as he goes along, but every now and then his inspiration fails him. Rather than commit the sin of silence, he sings *fal-al-deral*, *folderol*, or some similar gobbledygook. It was the medieval equivalent of *la-la-la*. From *being* a nonsense word it came to *mean* nonsense words."

He's so medicated that we can't understand a word he's saying; it's all folderol.

forbear/forebear

As a verb, *forbear* means to hold back from or resist. Your *fore-bears* are your ancestors, but just to be confusing, the alternate spelling is *forbears*, which means you can use either spelling to mean ancestor, but only *forbear* as a verb.

Forbear taunting the hamster; he's easily excitable.

My forebears are from Italy, where olive oil is almost a beverage.

forego/forgo

To *forego* is to go before, usually heard in its adjective form, *foregone*. Western Carolina University reported that one of its students would "forego his senior basketball year," which means that he would go before his senior basketball year, which makes very little sense. I don't know what it is about college sports that invites this error, but the Official College

Sports Network also reported that a Michigan State goaltender would "forego his senior season." The verb they both meant to use was *forgo:* to do without.

Putting on your socks foregoes putting on your shoes.

I would have to forgo my doughnut tonight to stick to my New Year's resolution; thank goodness I had my fingers crossed on New Year's Eve.

forensic

"Police forces have medical and scientific departments often described as departments of forensic medicine and forensic science. Policemen tend to refer to the people working in these departments as the *forensic specialists* and then extend this use to the departments themselves, referring to them as *forensics*," says *Baronage* editor Frederick Hogarth. "Detectives pick up an exhibit, place it in a plastic bag, and then hand it to a subordinate with the order, 'Take that to forensics.' As a consequence of reading this in novels and hearing it on television and radio, many of the public (and the police) have come to believe that *forensic* means 'scientific' or 'medical.' It does not. *Forensic* means 'legal.' It has never meant anything other than 'legal' or 'appropriate or adapted to argument.'"

After studying the forensic evidence, the judge tossed out the case of the cat owner who sued the dog owner for her cat's mental duress.

foreword

I'll hold back from embarrassing my colleagues, but this word is often misspelled, even by authors. A *foreword* is the short introductory statement at the beginning of a book, usually written by a person other than the book's author. It's not a *forward* or a *forword*. Think of it as the *word*s that go be*fore* the book.

I asked Kim Basinger to write the foreword for my book, but her "people" told me she was unavailable.

forgo *see* **forego**

former/latter

The terms *latter* and *former* should only be used when you're talking about a list of two things or people. If I say, "I have two cars: a station wagon and a sports car," then the former is the station wagon and the latter is the sports car. If you're using a list of more than two things, then *latter* and *former* can only serve to confuse. Instead, say *last* and *first*.

Brad went on dates with Alyssa and Karen, and said the former had an annoying laugh.

I have a blue dress and a red dress, and wearing the latter always helps me attract eligible men.

forte

Here's a pronunciation lesson that shocked me: *Forte* is pronounced "fort," not "for-tay!" *Forte* is another word we've borrowed from the French. It means strength, as in a person's strong suit.

I'm not surprised that he won the talent contest; swallowing fire while riding a unicycle has always been his forte.

forth/fourth

Forth means onward or forward. *Fourth* comes after third.

Go forth and conquer.

I came in fourth place in the pickle-eating contest.

fortissimo

Fortissimo is a musical term that means very loud.

Play fortissimo when you get to the chorus of "Mony Mony."

fortnight

Those wacky British and Australian people couldn't just say "two weeks," could they? Nooo. They had to employ their own special word, *fortnight*, just to flummox Americans. Okay, maybe it wasn't a dastardly plan. But *fortnight*, a contraction of *fourteen nights*, is a period of two weeks. *Fortnightly* means occurring every two weeks.

The e-zine is published fortnightly, so in each edition, you can expect two weeks' worth of news about stupid criminals.

fortuitous/fortunate

Fortuitous simply means happening by chance or accident. It does not mean a "happy accident"; the outcome of a fortuitous event can be good or bad. It is not a synonym for *fortunate*, which means lucky.

It was fortuitous that the disc jockey played my ex-husband's favorite song at my second wedding.

It's fortunate that you have dental insurance, because you have eighteen cavities.

fourscore

"Fourscore and seven years ago . . . " Four*what*? We've all heard the Gettysburg Address—in fact, we may have recited it back in grade school. But how many of us know that a *score*, in this context, means twenty, and therefore, *fourscore* is eighty (four times twenty)?

Fourscore years ago, my hair was brown instead of gray.

fourth *see* forth

free

Don't ever give anything away *for free*. You can give it away for nothing, but you'd be guilty of bad grammar if you gave it "for free." *Free* is an adjective, not an object. Give it *freely* instead.

When Victor handed out free chocolates to his coworkers on Halloween, his menopausal boss got in line five times.

freelance

Freelance is one word (not *free lance*). Someone who free-lances is called a *freelancer*.

Freelance writers are rarely wealthy people.

fulsome

Fulsome praise is not a good thing! *Fulsome* does not mean plentiful; it means fake, disgusting, or overdone. If someone gives you fulsome praise, he or she is blowing sunshine up your wazoo. I don't think the British newspaper *The Guardian* real-ized this when they ran an article stating, "TV watchdogs have written to ITV, ITN and Sky News with fulsome praise of their coverage of the terrorist crisis."

I'm sure her fulsome praise was just intended to butter me up because she knows I could fire her.

fun

Fun is a noun. It is only a noun. There is no such thing as a *fun time*. You can say you had an enjoyable time, or that you had fun. Though it's become extremely common, try to remember not to use *fun* as an adjective ("he's a fun guy," "it's a fun place," "it was so fun," and so on). And for Pete's sake, don't ever let me see you use the un-word *funner*!

I had fun playing carnival games, even though I spent $60 and only wound up with a tiny stuffed tiger to show for it.

funky
In 1992, Beastie Boys member Mike D complained, "The fact is that *funky* is the most misused word in music today." That's probably because *funk* doesn't have an easy definition. Funk combines elements of jazz, rhythm & blues, and soul. According to Chris M. Slawecki, senior editor of AllAboutJazz.com, "In a typical four/four stomp, funk comes down hard on the 'one,' sure. And funk often uses such instruments as guitars and keyboards more rhythmically (like percussion) than melodically. But no two people would give you the same definition of funk."

George Clinton plays funky music.

further *see* **farther**

Gg

gadfly

A *gadfly* is a fly that pesters animals. An irritating person who tries the patience of others can also be called a *gadfly*.

The telemarketer quickly became a gadfly when she wouldn't let me get off the phone politely, so I began quoting Bible verses and she hung up on me.

gaffe/gaff

A *gaffe* is a potentially embarrassing social blunder. A *gaff* is what fishermen use to spear or lift fish, what workers use to climb to the top of a telephone pole, or a spur affixed to a gamecock's leg. *Gaff* is also a verb that refers to using a gaff to spear a fish or attach the spur to the gamecock.

I hope it wasn't a gaffe when I made fun of Dave Barry earlier in this book.

I tried to gaff the fish, but it got away.

gel/jell

I know you know what *gel* means; it's that stuff you use to style your hair. But did you know that when an idea comes together in your mind, it *jells*, not *gels*? To *jell* is to set (as in a liquid that thickens and hardens) or take form. To remember this, think of Jell-O, which is a liquid that sets into solid form.

The longer it's been since he washed his hair, the more gel he uses.

The two writers brainstormed until they had a short story that jelled.

gender/sex

Purists will tell you that *gender* refers to social roles (masculine and feminine) or whether a word is masculine or feminine in form, and that *sex* is the word you should use if you're referring to whether someone is biologically male or female. As a society, we have a fear of using the word *sex*, which is probably why *gender* started doing double duty.

In my house, we don't have typical gender roles; my husband does the cooking and I fix the car.

The sex of the baby is female.

gentleman

Just this morning, a reporter on NBC referred to an alleged serial killer as a *gentleman*. "The gentleman has been taken into custody," she said. Did she really mean that this was a gentle man? That's a little too polite for my taste.

The gentleman laid his coat over a puddle so I could walk across it; then he got bronchitis from walking around with a wet coat for the rest of the night.

ghostwriter

Nope, a *ghostwriter* doesn't write about ghosts. He or she is the usually uncredited writer who is hired to write under someone else's byline—or under no byline at all. Ghostwriters are commonly used for celebrities' autobiographies.

I would love to be hired to ghostwrite Tom Cruise's biography, because that would mean he'd actually have to talk to me.

gibe *see* jibe

gift

Free gift is a redundant phrase. If someone tries to make you pay for a gift, this is a bad person. All gifts are, by definition, free.

The bank is offering a toaster as a gift when you open an account.

gormless *see* feckless

gourmand/gourmet

Both gourmand and gourmet describe a person who has fine taste in food and drink; however, gourmand can also describe a person who is gluttonous. To avoid confusion, I'd advise sticking to gourmet when you intend to compliment and gourmand when you intend to insult. Also, gourmet is not an adjective. Real estate ads that boast about "gourmet kitchens" could be reworded to read "kitchen fit for a gourmet," or "a gourmet's kitchen."

Because Pierre is a gourmet, I asked for his advice about side dishes to serve with my macaroni and cheese.

Hide the refrigerator! My uncle Edgar is coming, and he's quite a gourmand.

grammar

I'm always horrified when someone who purports to be a writer spells this word *grammer.* If you promise not to tell her I told you this, one of my book editors (not this one!) asked me to write a section of "grammer tips." The correct spelling is *grammar.*

I always ask a writer friend to check my grammar before I send my work to editors.

grandam/grandame/grande dame

A *grandam* or *grandame* is a grandmother or old woman. A *grande dame* (pronounced *gron' dom'*) is a remarkable woman, usually elderly, who is well known in a particular field or is highly esteemed.

Every time I see my grandam, she asks when I'm going to find myself a rich man to marry.

Amy Dunstin is the grande dame of the women's knitting circle.

gratuitous

Sure, you've heard people talk about "gratuitous sex scenes," but are you sure of what they meant? *Gratuitous* means unwarranted; without a justifiable reason for existing.

Erma didn't need to go to Hawaii for business; she was just taking a gratuitous trip.

grisly/gristly/grizzly

Grisly is hideous and horrible. *Gristly* describes meat that's full of gristle, the chewy white stuff. *Grizzly* is a type of bear, or an adjective that means gray. The Los Angeles County Sheriff's Department details a "grizzly murder" on its Web site—neither bears nor the color gray were responsible.

Beth needed fifty stitches after a grisly attack by an unidentified ferret.

This meat is too gristly for me, but my dog doesn't seem to mind it.

I hope to never encounter a grizzly bear.

gross/net

When you're talking money, *gross* is the amount before any deductions (expenses), and *net* is what's left after the deductions.

Two percent of the company's gross goes toward the "Give a D-student a Second Chance" college fund.

The author receives 10 percent of the net sales on her book.

grow

Please don't *grow* nonliving things. Your business can grow, but you can't grow it. Neither can you grow your bank account or your investments. Instead, try the words *expand* or *increase*.

I grow grapes in my garden because I'm too cheap to buy wine.

guffaw

My sister used to make fun of my mom for using the word *guffaw*. She maintained that no one else in the world ever used the word. Prove her wrong by using it. To *guffaw* is to laugh uproariously.

Trying to hold back my laughter during the sex education lecture didn't work; I just ended up guffawing even louder.

gyp

I once wrote a letter to a writer friend of mine explaining that I was worried someone was going to think I'd *gypped* him (ripped him off). She wrote back, "I don't consider myself a super politically correct person, and I'm sure you didn't even give it a second thought because it's been in American usage for a long time, but be careful with the word *gypped*. It's pejorative to Romany people commonly referred to as *gypsies*. It's like saying 'Indian-giver,' 'Jewing someone,' etc."

Hh

HIV
HIV stands for "human immunodeficiency virus." Therefore, don't call it the *HIV virus* unless you like repeating yourself. As I was writing this, I heard a newscaster ask, "Why is the deadly HIV virus spreading?" And *AIDS* stands for *Acquired Immunodeficiency Syndrome*, so don't call it the *AIDS syndrome*.

hacker *see* **cracker**

halcyon
I got a letter from one of my old college buddies, and she referred to our college days as "the halcyon years." I admit it—I had to look up the word. *Halcyon* means carefree or flourishing. People generally use the word to refer to profitable or happy years.

I often look back on the halcyon years before I had a mortgage, when I could spend $200 a week on new clothes.

hanged/hung

People are *hanged*. Things are *hung*. Oh, okay, okay, all you pervs. If you're a slang fan, certain well-endowed males can be described as *hung*, too. Or so I hear.

If he is found guilty, he will be hanged.

I hung the sprig of mistletoe over the doorway to my office, but it must have been a dud because I never got kissed.

hangnail

Oddly enough, a *hangnail* isn't a nail that's hanging off. Instead, it's a piece of skin that's separated around the side or base of the fingernail.

I can't come to work today; I have a hangnail.

ha'penny

Dating back to about 1550, a *ha'penny* is a contraction for a halfpenny.

I enjoy the Muppets' rendition of the song "Christmas Is Coming": "If you haven't got a penny, a ha'penny will do . . ."

harbinger

If someone calls you a "harbinger of good fortune," do you know what he or she is telling you? A harbinger is a sign; a predictor or foreshadow. Lucky you to be a sign of good fortune!

My creaking knee is a harbinger of rain.

ha...

hark/hawk/hock

You can *hawk* or *hock* your wares. To *hawk* them is to sell them; to *hock* is to pawn them (trade in). To *hawk* is also to clear your throat, and to be *in hock* is to be in debt. To *hark* is to pay attention.

The street merchants hawked their "Bolex" watches to passersby.

I had to hock my wedding ring to pay my cell phone bill.

Hark, this information will be on your exam.

headquarter

Headquarter is not a verb. You can have your headquarters in Boston, but your office is not *headquartered* there.

The tweezer manufacturing company's headquarters are on Market Street.

healthy/healthful

There's no such thing as a *healthy* lunch. *Healthy* means having good health. You can be healthy, your heart can be healthy, or your dog can be healthy, but your food is *healthful:* bringing about good health.

The doctor had to repeatedly assure the hypochondriac that she was a healthy young woman.

We banned smoking in our office to promote a healthful working environment, so now the receptionist chews her tobacco.

hear/listen

The difference between *hearing* and *listening* is that listening requires effort. Hearing is a passive activity.

I know you can hear me, but sometimes I think you're not listening to me when I talk about how my cat is psychically attuned to my emotions.

hellacious

Is it just me, or does everyone assume that *hellacious* means awful? Well, according to all of the dictionaries I consulted, *hellacious* actually means a few things, only one of which is "awful." The other meanings are: extremely strong, huge, difficult, and great (I know—hellacious is one of those weird words that has two meanings that are antonyms!).

After riding his motorcycle through a hellacious sandstorm, Franklin had to have his nostrils professionally cleaned.

hemiplegic/paraplegic/quadriplegic

A *hemiplegic* person is paralyzed on one side of the body. A *paraplegic* is paralyzed in the lower half of the body (including the legs). A *quadriplegic* has paralysis of all four limbs.

herewith

Usually seen when a person encloses something with a letter, *herewith* means just what it sounds like: here with (this);

enclosed. It also means hereby, though I'm not altogether sure why we need another word for hereby.

Herewith, you'll find photos of the banana slugs I've been studying in New York.

hermaphrodite *see* **androgenous**

highfalutin
This informal word, which means pompous or self-important, doesn't need an apostrophe at the end of it. There is no "g" at the end that is intentionally deleted. (Well, it *can* be spelled with a "g," too, but it doesn't have to be.)

The down-to-earth people in our book club don't appreciate the newcomer's highfalutin attitude. She suggests our romance novels are nothing but junk and recommends we begin reading more plays by Shakespeare.

hilarious *see* **hysterical**

historic/historical
If it makes history or is likely to be studied years from now, it's *historic*, not *historical*! I always cringe when I hear about a "historical speech" made by the current president. If it were a historical speech, then he would have made it years ago. *Historical* means part of history, or pertaining to the study of history.

In a historic decision, the coach allowed a woman to be on the all-male football team, and the woman later won the title of Most Valuable Player.

The homeowners found valuable historical documents, which were appraised at $1,000,000 on Antiques Roadshow, *buried in a locked box under their swingset.*

hoard/horde

A *horde* is a crowd—usually a rambunctious one—and a *hoard* is a stash. To hoard something is to save it, or to keep it hidden.

There was such a horde waiting for free beer that we gave up and went home.

She hoarded beauty products in the hopes that she'd look young forever.

hock *see* hark

hold

If you have something in your hand, you're *holding* it. It has also recently become acceptable to use *hold* in relation to something intangible, such as a world record.

Whenever I hold my teddy bear, I think about the boy who gave it to me in the fifth grade.

ho...

home/hone

When you want to focus in on something (or zero in), the correct expression is to *home in*, not to *hone in*. To *hone* is to perfect or to sharpen.

The bachelor homed in on his target: a buxom brunette.

My neighbor honed his pruning shears and spent the next three hours hacking his shrubs.

Billy honed his basketball skills by taking shots at his wastebasket across the room.

homely

In Britain and Ireland, *homely* is a synonym for *homey*, meaning comfortable. It's a compliment. Quite a departure from what it means in American English: plain or unsophisticated, usually insinuating that someone is ugly. And did you ever notice that you almost never hear a man described as *homely*? We women bear the brunt of it. Well, I'll be darned if I'm going to go along with that . . .

Quit setting me up on blind dates with homely men.

homicide *see* assassination

homonym

Homonyms are words that sound alike and may be spelled alike but have different meanings.

Right (correct) and right (the opposite of left) are homonyms, as are know (comprehend) and no (the opposite of yes).

hone *see* **home**

hopefully
I am hopefully about to tell you the correct use of *hopefully*. *Hopefully* means filled with hope. I am filled with hope that you will learn that *hopefully* does *not* mean "I hope," "we hope," or "it is hoped." Generally, when you see the word *hopefully* as the first word in a sentence, it is being used incorrectly. For example: "Hopefully, our team will win the game." Does the speaker really mean that the team will win the game while filled with hope? I think not. The correct way to say it is "We hope our team will win the game," plain and simple.

Miss Piggy gazed at Kermit hopefully, thinking this would be the perfect moment for him to propose.

horde *see* **hoard**

hung *see* **hanged**

hysterical/hilarious
"You should have seen what he did with those hamburger buns—it was hysterical!" my friend tells me. The word that

has escaped my friend here is *hilarious*. If something is *hysterical*, it is experiencing a spell of hysteria—loss of control over its emotions. In other words, a thing can't be *hysterical*. A person can be *hysterical*, but this use comes with a warning: "The comedian was hysterical" is wrong, unless, of course, the comedian was going through an outrageous emotional outburst in which he lost control.

She was so hysterical about winning the lottery that the doctor had to sedate her.

I thought it was hilarious when my little brother told the famous artist that he should learn how to color inside the lines.

Ii

ID

Short for *identification*, ID doesn't need any periods (what would the "d" stand for?).

I'm offended that convenience store clerks have stopped asking for my ID when I buy alcohol. Yes, I know I'm forty-seven.

id *see* ego

ignorant

"I would appreciate it very much if you could help with a crusade of mine," writes Mary M. Boldish. "When I hear people use the word *ignorant* to describe someone who is rude or uncouth it makes me cringe." Me too, Mary. The word *ignorant* means unaware, or demonstrating a dearth of knowledge.

I was ignorant of your fear of peanut butter; please pardon me for serving you a peanut butter and jelly sandwich.

ilk

"*Ilk* is a much misused word," says Frederick Hogarth, editor of *Baronage* magazine (*www.baronage.co.uk*). "One often hears phrases such as 'others of that ilk,' especially among politicians, supposedly meaning 'others of that kind.' However, *ilk* means same, and accordingly, 'Anderson of that Ilk' means 'Anderson of that Same,' which in turn means 'Anderson of Anderson.' Some Scottish chiefs choose the latter style (e.g., Macleod of Macleod), while others choose the former (e.g., Moncreiffe of that Ilk)." *Ilk* refers to a person's name and his property's name being the same.

Hutchison of that Ilk isn't fond of lima beans.

illicit *see* elicit

immigrate *see* emigrate

imminent *see* eminent

immolate

Immolate doesn't inherently have anything to do with fire. To *immolate* is to kill an animal as a sacrifice, or to destroy. It doesn't have to be sacrificed in a fire.

The explorer discovered a tribe that immolated tarantulas to the god of the hunt.

immured/inured

A press release from the Gay and Lesbian Medical Association says, "In a community immured to the pain of loss, these new casualties are almost overlooked as being par for the course." Nope. *Immured* means entrapped or enclosed, and takes the preposition *in* or *within*. *Inured*, however, means accustomed, and takes the preposition *to*.

There's a fly immured in my ice cube!

The teacher was inured to hearing ridiculous excuses for late homework, but Sally's "My dog ate my computer" took the cake.

impact

Impact was born to be a noun. Don't try to make it do something it doesn't want to do, like become a verb, as in this line in the Poughkeepsie *Journal:* "The worlds of athletics and economics often team up in the Hudson Valley, as sports impact the economy." Nope. Sports *affect* the economy. An *impact* is a forceful contact or a strong influence.

My mother's teachings had such an impact on me that even now, at age twenty-seven, I can't cross the street without asking a stranger to hold my hand.

impair/impede

To *impair* is to handicap, limit, make more difficult, or make worse. To *impede* is to hold (something) back, stand in the way, or thwart.

You're impairing my weight-loss efforts by putting this chocolate cake under my nose.

The glut of paperwork we had to fill out to obtain permits impeded our efforts to quickly film the movie Attack of the Killer Rutabagas.

impassible/impassable

You are impervious to pain or harm, or not showing any emotion (especially appearing not to care or sympathize) if you are *impassible*. *Impassable* means it can't be passed (for example, a blocked road or bridge).

I told my boss that I needed some time off to grieve the death of my goldfish, Herbert, but my boss was impassible, telling me to "flush it down the toilet and get a grip."

The cattle were mating in the middle of the street, making it impassable.

impassive

Just like *impassible*, if you are *impassive*, you're not showing any emotion, especially in a situation where you would be expected to have strong emotions. *Impassive* is not a description for an impasse (a deadlock).

He had just been awarded the Nobel Prize, and yet he appeared impassive, shrugging and asking, "So what's for lunch?"

impeach
President Clinton was impeached for perjury in front of a grand jury. Did that mean he left office? Nope. People frequently make the mistake of thinking that *impeachment* means getting kicked out of office. *Impeachment* is simply a formal accusation before a tribunal that a public official has behaved improperly. The official may then be acquitted or convicted by legislative vote. You may also hear that a witness has been *impeached* in court; that means the witness's testimony has been found to be incredible.

Andrew Johnson was the first U.S. President to be impeached, but he was acquitted by one vote in the Senate.

impede *see* **impair**

impertinence/pertinence
Writer Denise Mainquist was confused when an editor thanked her for her *pertinence*. "I had to think about this for several days," she says. "I believe this man may consider *pertinence* to be the opposite of *impertinence*." Poor misguided editor. *Impertinence* means insolence or rudeness. *Pertinence*, however, means relevance.

I was shocked by his impertinence; did you hear him tell me I had split ends?

I don't see the pertinence of his cross-dressing habits to our current business discussions.

impetus/impetuous

An *impetus* is a motivator, stimulus, or inclination. It can also mean the reaction to such a motivation or stimulus. Someone who is *impetuous* is impulsive; *impetuous* also describes a powerful or violent rush.

She lacked the impetus to get out of bed, so she stayed under the covers and prayed her kids wouldn't set the house on fire during the next few hours.

The impetuous musician bought expensive saxophones the way other people buy socks.

imply/infer

According to writer Jerry Hatchett, "Folks often say, 'Are you *inferring* that I did that?' when they mean *imply*." To *imply* is to suggest without saying something outright; to *infer* is to interpret or deduce based on something that is not said or shown outright.

When he asked if I thought my blouse looked more snug than usual, I think he was implying that I'm eating too many doughnuts.

When my bumbling brother came home in the middle of the day, I inferred that he had been fired again.

impregnable

Well, yes, one of its meanings is "able to be impregnated," but this word also means so secure as to be impenetrable (usually used to describe a building) or unassailable. In the latter sense, something that is *impregnable* is not subject to dispute.

Now that I've installed an alarm system, security cameras, and triple dead-bolt locks, I hope the kids' tree fort is impregnable.

impromptu *see* **extemporaneous**

inane
When something is utterly brainless, trivial, or pointless, it may be *inane*.

I listened to a couple having an inane argument about canned peas on the subway this afternoon.

inchoate
Here's a word we should use more often. Something is *inchoate* if it's in its formative stage, or if it's not fully realized or fleshed out.

My invention of a flushable cat toilet is inchoate; I still need to perfect its design and get my cat to use it.

incidental *see* **accidental**

include
Let's say you write the following sentence: "I've lived in many

places, including Boston, Greenville, Los Angeles, and Miami."
That's fine if you've also lived in other cities. However, if that's
the entire list of cities, then don't use the word *including*. Skip
the word altogether, like so: "I've lived in many places: Boston,
Greenville, Los Angeles, and Miami." *Include* is just for partial
lists.

*My pet peeves include people who lie and say they're not
contagious when they are, masochistic shaving devices, and
clothes that are "dry clean only."*

inclusion/mainstreaming
"'I believe in full inclusion for my child.' I hear this phrase
frequently. Usually the person saying it really means 'full-
mainstreaming.' This is one of my pet peeves. Inclusion and
mainstreaming are not the same thing!" says Tim Weiss, assistant director of PARENTS, Inc. "*Mainstreaming* is the placement of a child [with disabilities] in a 'regular' classroom,
usually in the child's neighborhood. *Inclusion* is the act of
ensuring that the child is able to benefit from and participate
in all activities, to the maximum extent possible, just as children without disabilities."

*To help with the boy's inclusion, the physical education
teacher provided a tee for him to use when playing baseball.*

*The boy with Down syndrome was mainstreamed in his
school district.*

incredible

I don't think people are really thinking when they say things like "He's an incredible person," or "That was an incredible presentation." If you think about the word *incredible* literally, it means not credible; not able to be believed. If the person is not credible, then he's probably not the nifty guy you're trying to say he is.

I found her explanation about the dog eating her homework to be incredible; she doesn't even have a dog.

incredulous *see* credible

incumbent

The *incumbent* politician is the one who's already in office. *Incumbent* also means essential or mandatory and is usually followed by *on* or *upon*.

John felt it was incumbent on him to give little Ashley's pet turtle a proper burial in the backyard.

indigenous

Indigenous means native; originating in the place specified.

Are monkeys indigenous to this country, or were they introduced from another country?

indolence/insolence

Indolence is laziness. *Insolence* is the act of being cheeky, offensive, or conceited, or not respecting authority.

She proved her indolence by walking away from the table without even clearing her own plate.

He proved his insolence by sneaking out of the house while he was grounded.

ineffable

If it's *ineffable*, it's either beyond words or taboo.

I got ineffable pleasure from watching my daughter beat that baton-twirler in the talent contest.

Sex was an ineffable topic in my parents' home; until I was twenty-one, I thought babies came from storks.

inextricable/inexplicable

Use *inextricable* when you mean that something is hopelessly entwined, unable to be unconnected, or impossible to get out of, literally or figuratively. *Inextricable* can also mean unavoidable. *Inexplicable* means not able to be explained.

When the kitten finished mauling my yarn, it was inextricably knotted.

How Fred, who has never passed a single science exam, ever got into medical school is inexplicable to me.

infamous/notorious
I was playing Scattegories with friends, and the category was *infamous people*. My friend proudly shouted, "Martin Luther King, Jr.!" Oops. *Infamous* is a description for someone who is famous in a bad way. Serial killers, members of the mob, and people embroiled in scandals may be *infamous*. (My friend didn't get a point for her answer, in case you were wondering.) *Notorious* is a synonym to *infamous*; it also describes someone who is known for something bad. Either word can also be used figuratively; a person doesn't need to be literally famous to be *notorious*; your mother may be notorious for being late, or your neighbor might be infamous for "borrowing" people's tools and not returning them, if those are well-known facts about them.

   Charles Manson is infamous.
   Leah is notorious for overcooking the Thanksgiving turkey.

infectious *see* **contagious**

infer *see* **imply**

inflammable *see* **flammable**

inquiry/query
If you have only one question, you have a *query*. An *inquiry* is a series of questions. In the writing profession, a *query letter* is a

pitch; it's a summary of an article, novel, screenplay, or other form of writing, plus the writer's biography and special qualifications. The writer uses this letter to try to sell his or her work to a publisher or producer, or to attract the attention of an agent.

The manager answered my query about the price of the ceramic pigs.

My boyfriend was subjected to an inquiry when I found out he had a tattoo that said "FiFi forever" on his arm.

insolence *see* **indolence**

insure *see* **ensure**

integral/intrical/intricate
This one's more of a pronunciation issue, but the word is *integral* (not *intrical*), referring to a necessary component. *Integral* can be pronounced with the emphasis on the first syllable (preferred) or the second syllable. Recently, when I got an acceptance letter from the Chicken Soup anthologies for one of my essays, it said, "Thank you for being an intricate part of the Chicken Soup family!" An intricate part? *Intricate* means designed in a complex way. I don't think I was a complicated part of the "Chicken Soup family." Rather, I was an *integral* part.

Tiffany failed to realize that getting the oil changed was an integral part of car ownership.

Ollie came up with an intricate plan to incriminate his brother.

Internet/intranet/World Wide Web
The *Internet* (capital "i") is the system of networks that connects computers worldwide. The *World Wide Web* (WWW) is one facet of the Internet; the WWW contains all of the Web pages in existence. The Internet also includes e-mail, file transfer, chat, etc. An *intranet* (lowercase "i") is a private network within a company or organization that's not available on the WWW.

When I got onto the Internet, I found seventeen e-mails from strangers who wanted to sell me a product to increase my bust size.

I surf the World Wide Web to get information about how to raise chinchillas.

Our company's intranet has information about our sales, our meetings schedule, and private memos.

intrical *or* intricate *see* integral

inundate
To *inundate* is to overload or overwhelm.

Because Tracy was inundated with work, she asked her husband to cook dinner, and he promptly ordered pizza.

in.

inured *see* **immured**

invalid

One of my neighbors ran an ambulance company. On the side of his trucks, it said "Invalid coach." I used to think, "Boy, that's pretty self-deprecating for him to advertise his company as not valid." You're probably sharper than I was, and have already figured out that it wasn't in-*val*-id, but rather *in*-va-lid. The latter pronunciation means someone who is disabled because of a medical condition.

She was an invalid after her stroke.

Voter confusion caused the Board of Election Commissioners to declare the computerized vote counts invalid.

invariable

Invariable means it never varies. I worked with a writer who was overly fond of the word invariably, using it to mean "almost always." "Writers send their work to the big agencies, only to be invariably rejected," he'd write. Really? If the writers were invariably rejected, the agencies wouldn't have any clients.

My alarm clock invariably rings at 8 A.M., and I invariably hurl it across the room and pull the covers over my head.

ironic

Thanks a lot, Alanis Morissette, for confusing the world even further about the word *irony*. The series of "ironies" in her song, "Ironic," such as rain on your wedding day and a 'no smoking' sign on your cigarette break, are just unfortunate coincidences. ("The good advice that you just didn't take" isn't even coincidental . . . but don't get me started.) Something *ironic* is not just coincidental; it has to poke fun at the human condition or express something that's precisely the opposite of what's reasonably expected.

In the song "Escape (The Piña Colada Song)," it's ironic that the man answers his wife's personals ad.

irregardless

There. Is. No. Such. Standard. Word. See how I did that? I put in lots of periods to get my point across. Please don't use this non-word or I will weep. The correct word is *regardless*.

Regardless of how late we are, I still have to curl my eyelashes.

it's/its

Use *it's* when you want a shorter way of saying *it is*. When you want to use the possessive form (belonging to it), there is no apostrophe. I often see sentences like "It's color is blue." It is color is blue? That makes no sense. Think of it this way: you wouldn't write *her's* or *his's*, would you?

It's a beautiful day in the neighborhood.

The plant grew too big for its pot, so I replanted it in the wastebasket.

iterate/reiterate

I didn't even know there was any such word as *iterate*, but when I learned that there was, I figured if *reiterate* meant to say again, then *iterate* meant to say. Nope. Oddly enough, *iterate* and *reiterate* mean the same thing, like *flammable* and *inflammable*. Both of them mean to repeat.

I iterated my policy against office romances because the first time I explained it, the secretary and the custodian were making out in the corner and didn't hear me.

Just to reiterate, you cannot miss more than five days of work per year, even if the custodian did give you mononucleosis.

Jj

jail/prison

Jail and *prison* aren't the same thing. *Jail* is the place where people who have committed lesser crimes are kept (usually for short sentences), and where people who are suspected of major crimes are held before they go to trial. If you're arrested for driving with a suspended license or public drunkenness, you'll probably go to jail. *Prison*, on the other hand, is for longer sentences and those who have committed more serious crimes. That's where convicts are kept after the trial is over.

Some people get upset that criminals have color televisions in prison, but really, where can you find a black-and-white television anymore?

jell *see* gel

jibe/jive/gibe

If we're going to use slang, let's at least get it right. When you say X *jibes* with Y, you mean that X is in agreement with Y, or coordinates with it. They don't *jive* with each other! *Jive* is a type of dance that was popular in the 1940s and 1950s, and it's a word for nonsensical talk or lies. A *gibe* (can also be spelled *jibe*) is an insulting statement.

His earlier excuse for not washing the dog doesn't jibe with the one he's giving me today.

Don't give me that jive about sleeping at your friend's house—I know you were at the horse track again!

My enemy made a nasty gibe about my poodle's new haircut.

junction/juncture

A *junction* is an intersection and a *juncture* is a particular point in time.

We live just past the junction of Prospect Street and Apple-gate Drive.

We have no comment at this juncture; we're waiting for the tabloids to pay us thousands of dollars for exclusive rights to our story.

juxtapose

When you *juxtapose* things, you place them near each other (literally or figuratively), usually to compare them.

Juxtaposing the wallpaper and the floor mat made me realize they didn't match at all.

Kk

kibbutz/kibitz

Kibitz is generally a negative word; to *kibitz* is to butt in with unsolicited advice or opinions. *Kibbutz* is a collective farm or settlement in Israel where children are reared communally.

We stopped inviting Maureen to our parties because she has a habit of kibitzing, especially to give us her opinions about the proper way to disinfect a toilet tank.

The children were brought up on a kibbutz.

kudos

Kudos is singular. Therefore, even though it may sound weird, you should treat it as a singular noun.

Kudos is due Jean Drummond for her excellent perform-ance of "Why Don't We Do It in the Road?" on the oboe.

lager *see* ale

landslide *see* avalanche

latter *see* former

lay/lie
Lay is a transitive verb, which means that it must take a direct object. You can't just *lay;* you have to lay *something*. (Okay, all of you with dirty minds, quit looking at me with that smirky face.) *Lie* is an intransitive verb, which means it doesn't take an object. You can *lie* down. You can't *lie* something. Now here's where it gets confusing: the past tense of *lie* is *lay*. So if you want to express that you were lying on the couch this morning, you can say that you *lay* there. The past tense of *lay* is *laid*. You can say that you laid the newspaper on the table.

I was taught in school that people *lie* and inanimate objects *lay*. This is wrong! (With all my poor education, isn't it amazing that I'm so darn intelig . . . intelleg . . . smart?) Objects don't lay. They just lie. (An inanimate object can't pick something up and put it down somewhere, so it can't *lay* anything.) Remember that you must specify what is being laid if you want to use the word *lay*. A chicken can lay an egg. Handymen can lay tiles. (Ask yourself, what is being laid? An egg and tiles.) But a cat just lies on the floor, and a box of doughnuts lies on the counter.

A quick way to remember the difference: When you lay something, you place it. There's an "a" in *lay* and an "a" in *place*. *Lie* means to recline. There's an "i" in *lie* and an "i" in *recline*.

Katy lays the pizza on the dining room table and waits for her vulturelike children to scarf it down.

Steven lies on his bed and contemplates his navel.

(Past tense) Irving was so drunk that he lay in the hallway.

(Past tense) Lauren laid the blackmail photos on the coffee table and laughed maniacally.

lead

The past tense of the verb *lead* is *led*, not *lead*. I think the confusion stems from the verb *read*, whose past tense is *read*.

The head munchkin led the way to the yellow brick road.

lectern/podium/pulpit

You stand *on* a *podium*. That's the little step that's usually behind a *lectern*, which is the raised desk or stand that a speaker uses, where he or she can place notes. In a church, a lectern is usually called a *pulpit*.

> *I stood on the podium to give my speech about raising wombats. I placed my index cards on the lectern.*

> *The preacher stood behind the pulpit to give his sermon, "Facing Sinners Without Barriers."*

lend/loan

Loan is a noun, not a verb. You can't *loan* someone money—you have to *lend* it to him or her. You can make a loan, though.

> *Can I have a loan until payday?*

> *Why do I never learn not to lend my sister my favorite clothes?*

lens

There is no "e" at the end of *lens*, whether you're talking about a contact lens, camera lens, or otherwise.

> *Isabella dropped her contact lens on the dance floor during the Chicken Dance.*

less *see* fewer

lessee/lessor

The *lessor* is the one who leases property to someone. The person who receives the property in exchange for payment is the *lessee*. For words like these, think of *employer* and *employee*. The employer is the one who gives employment, and the employee is the one who gets employment.

The lessor handed me the keys to my new car.

I am the proud lessee of a Rent-A-Wreck castoff.

levity

The primary meaning of *levity* is lightness, especially in mood or manner when it seems out of place. It can also mean fickleness or inconsistency.

He showed such levity after he was fired; he did a jig and said he was going to go to Disney World.

liable/likely/apt

Liable means to be obligated or responsible (for something). You can also use it to mean prone to experience something negative, but if you're suggesting something positive, the better word choice is *apt*. *Apt* is also used to suggest a habit—if you're apt to be late, it means you're habitually late. *Likely* doesn't necessarily suggest a habit; if you're likely to be late, it may mean that you're habitually late, or it may mean that because of heavy traffic or bad weather conditions, it is reasonable to assume that you might be late, even if you're usually on time.

No, you can't take little Jimmy to the park to help you woo women. I'm the baby sitter, so I'm liable for him.

Mary has been complaining about her long hair all week, so I think it's likely that she'll get a haircut.

libel *see* **defamation**

lie *see* **lay**

likely *see* **liable**

line
You would be well advised not to use the word *line* as a substitute for *kind*, as in "What's your line of work?" Even though some dictionaries accept this usage, many grammarians don't like it. Might as well stick to *kind* or *type* in this scenario.
What kind of work do you do?
The drunken man couldn't walk a straight line.

listen *see* **hear**

literally *see* **figuratively**

live
"People have been broadcasting *live* for a hundred years, but the meaning has been slowly changing," says writer Lawrence Benedict. "Yesterday, I read that people who are broadcasting

streaming video on the Web have resorted to using the phrase *live-live* to mean that viewers will actually be seeing what is going on at the moment it is going on, real-time, as opposed to some very sophisticated manipulations that pass for live, and are often believed to be live by the viewer.

"Practically everything that appears live is actually recorded. 'Live' radio talk shows record the callers and create a delay in the playback allowing editors to remove unwanted comments or inappropriate trains of thought. Even though the delay is only a few seconds, it has the same effect as if it were a hundred years. The content can be manipulated and the listeners even tricked, if that were the producers' intent. David Letterman is 'recorded live' (what would the alternative be?). It plays across the country in the same time slot. Yet we ignore the 'recorded' part because it appears so live (usually).

"'Live motion video' is a complete departure from 'live.' That phrase means a recording playing back at a high enough frame rate to appear live to the viewers, although the viewers, in this case, are fully aware that they are watching a recording."

We were thrilled to see a live performance of Bubble Boy.

livid

You probably know *livid* as a word for very angry, but did you know it has another meaning, too? Not only that, but its *original* meaning is "bluish," and is used to describe a black-and-blue bruise. Oddly, it can also mean pale, used to describe someone who looks sickly.

Davey the Daredevil had livid bruises after he dove off his motorcycle into a vat of empty film canisters.

loan *see* **lend**

loath/loathe
Loath is reluctant or averse. You can be *loath* (an adjective); you can't be *loathe* (a verb). To *loathe* is to hate.

I am loath to spend so much money on shoes for the wedding; when else am I going to wear puce pumps?

I loathe the hiccups because once I get them, I can never seem to get rid of them.

loose/lose
This is one of those spelling errors that drives me crazy. I think people know the difference between the meanings of *loose* (the opposite of tight) and *lose* (the opposite of find), yet nearly every day, I read about someone *loosing* weight, *loosing* their keys, or *loosing* their mind. No! That word is *losing*.

These pants are too loose on me; maybe I should eat some more doughnuts.

I used to lose my car in the mall parking lot; now I just look for the inflatable doll I tied to the back bumper.

loquacious

Someone who is *loquacious* is too talkative; long-winded. Something that is *loquacious* (like a book or letter) is too wordy.

The new minister is so loquacious that my husband takes his radio with earphones to church.

The Bakers' annual Christmas letter is always loquacious; this year it contained sixteen pages about their eldest daughter's winning soccer goal.

lothario

A *lothario* is a "Don Juan"—someone who lives to charm women; a womanizer.

I know you think he's in love with you, but be careful— I think he's a bit of a lothario.

luxuriant/luxurious

Luxuriant is the adjective to use if you're talking about something that's growing thickly and/or plentifully. It's usually used to describe vegetation, hair, or fur. Its corresponding noun is *luxuriance*. *Luxurious* is the word if you're talking about something that seems expensive, extravagant, or of rich quality. Its corresponding nouns are *luxury* and *luxuriousness*.

I'm jealous of Susan's luxuriant hair.

We couldn't afford the luxurious whirlpool tub, so we poured water and bubbles into the kids' wading pool and jumped in.

Mm

magick

If you see the word *magick*, chances are it has to do with the Wiccan religion. Wiccans don't want their spells to be confused with garden-variety parlor tricks and sleight of hand, so they added on the *k* to set their particular brand of magic apart.

If my magick works, my ex-boyfriend will soon be begging me to come back to him.

mainstreaming *see* **inclusion**

majority/plurality

If you have achieved a *majority*, you've gotten at least half of the votes. If you have a *plurality*, then you got more votes than any other candidate, even though you may not have achieved more than half of all votes.

Because Maggie got 60 votes out of 100 votes cast, she won the majority.

Irv got 25 votes, Eileen got 30 votes, and Josh got 35 votes, so Josh has a plurality.

malapropism

Well, since this book is full of them, I figured it was only fair that I define the word *malapropism*, which means the incorrect use of a word. The word comes from the play *The Rivals* (1775), written by Richard Brinsley Sheridan. In it, an over-the-top comic character named Mrs. Malaprop consistently misused and abused perfectly good words, trying to sound educated and failing miserably.

When Bob said, "You're an ungrateful wrench," that was a malapropism. He meant to say "ungrateful wench."

malignant *see* benign

man

How *man* got to be a verb is beyond me. But especially in this era of political correctness, it seems a little odd to have women *manning* a booth, a desk, or a store. Substitute a real verb instead, like *running* or *working*.

Having a seventy-year-old woman running the kissing booth didn't attract many teenage customers.

I sprayed pepper spray at the strange man who was kneeling down in back of my car in the parking lot, and then I noticed he was just trying to fix my flat tire.

manslaughter *see* **assassination**

mastermind

This word is a compliment! When, oh, when will newscasters stop referring to common criminals as *masterminds*? You're not likely to call a bank robber a genius, and yet, we don't complain when they're called *masterminds*—very intelligent and creative people with the ability to plan or carry out complex operations. If they were so intelligent, why did they need to rob banks, anyway?

Earl was the mastermind of the winning science fair project.

may *see* **can**

mean *see* **average**

media

Media is plural (like *data*). Television is not *a media*. It's a *medium*.

The media are taking an interest in my neighbor's million-dollar birdbath.

median *see* **average**

mediate *see* **arbitrate**

medium *see* **clairaudient**

melee
A *melee* is an uncontrolled crowd or a group fight.

During the melee in the stands when our team lost the World Series, someone stole my wallet.

memento/momento
There is no such standard word as *momento*. A *memento* is a souvenir. Yet even respected members of the media pronounce it as if it were spelled *momento*.

Virginia took a matchbook as a memento of the hotel where they stayed on their honeymoon; Cletus took the maid's phone number.

mendacity/mendicity
Mendacity is the condition of being a liar, or the lie itself. *Mendicity* is the practice of begging.

I accused George of mendacity because I found out he never went to Yale even though he wrote on his résumé that he was an alumnus.

The only way the homeless man could get enough money to eat at the sushi restaurant was through mendicity.

me...

mercenary

For the longest time, I thought a *mercenary* was someone who showed mercy. Nay, it describes someone who is concerned only with money. A *mercenary* can also be a soldier who fights on the side of whoever pays him.

Some would say that lawyers are a mercenary lot; after taking out thousands of dollars in student loans, most lawyers are eager to make back their money.

The United States hired foreign mercenaries during wars against England and France.

meretricious/meritorious

Something *meretricious* sounds believable but is actually false or incorrect. *Meretricious* can also describe a relation with prostitutes. *Meritorious* means having merit; being worthy of commendation.

It turns out that the Publishers Clearinghouse was being meretricious when they told me the Prize Patrol was going to be in my area to award their big prize. Somehow they ended up clear across the country.

Lisa's meritorious speech, "Our Friends, The Cows," persuaded many people to become vegetarians.

metaphor/simile

A metaphor is a comparison that doesn't use *like* or *as*. A simile uses *like* or *as*.

> *"Men are pigs" is a metaphor.*
> *"Men are like pigs" is a simile.*

methodology

Methodology is the study of methods, or the entire set of methods and practices particular to a specific job or task. Many people use the word *methodology* when *method* or *methods* would be correct instead. (Again, that false belief that big words are better.) Incorrect: "The politician's methodology for dealing with the crisis was to lie about it." Correct: "The politician's method for dealing with the crisis was to lie about it."

> *You may question the doctor's methodology, but it's hard to dispute his results.*

midget *see* dwarf

millennium *see* century

minor/miner

An underage person is a *minor*. A person who works in a mine is a *miner*.

> *Don't give that minor any wine!*

The nation watched hopefully as the Quecreek miners were pulled to safety.

misanthrope

A *misanthrope* isn't just a misfit; he or she is someone who hates other people and avoids their company.

Ebeneezer Scrooge was a misanthrope of the first degree; he couldn't even stand his own family.

mischievous

It is not "mischievious." It's not spelled with an "i" after the "v," and it's not pronounced with an "i." It's just plain *mischievous*, which, of course, means rascally or troublemaking.

The mischievous children stole the doctor's stethoscope and tongue depressors.

misnomer

A *misnomer* isn't just a mistake. It's a name that doesn't befit what it describes. For example, a frozen TV dinner that's named "Exquisite Feast" may be a misnomer. It can also refer to calling someone or something by an incorrect name.

Bill's wife, Susan, heard him mumble the name "Olivia" in his sleep. Two days later, his attorney told Susan's divorce lawyer that it was just an innocent misnomer.

misogynist

By definition, a *misogynist* is someone who hates women. However, if you pay attention to the way some feminist groups throw around the word, you might believe it applies to anyone who doesn't agree with everything they say. *Misogynist* is a strong term and should only be used when the subject truly demonstrates a hatred of women. In case you're wondering, there is a word for someone who hates men: it's *misandrist*, and maybe it should be used more often!

Louis is such a misogynist that he wouldn't even allow his male friends to bring their wives to his house.

mnemonic

Do you remember *mnemonic devices* from grade school? *Mnemonic* can be a noun or an adjective, and it refers to those little "tricks" you use to remember something—for example, making up a short rhyme or using the initials of everything from a list in a sentence. To remember the notes that appear on the lines of a musical staff, many young musicians are taught the sentence "Every good boy does fine" (to represent the notes E, G, B, D, and F). That's a mnemonic.

"Roy G. Biv" is a mnemonic device to remember the colors of the rainbow: red, orange, yellow, green, blue, indigo, and violet.

momento *see* **memento**

moot/mute

A *moot* point frequently gets mangled into a *mute* point. (If the point were mute, no one would have heard it, anyway.) *Mute* means unable to speak, or refers to a tool used to quiet the sound of a musical instrument. But what's worse is this: The adjective *moot* has contradictory meanings. Most people today use it to describe something that's pointless to debate. However, moot also means debatable! Therefore, if you say, "Whether or not Mr. Klein is qualified for the job is moot," people may interpret it two ways: Either it doesn't matter whether Mr. Klein is or isn't qualified (maybe because he's the only person who will do the job), or it's questionable whether he's qualified or not (and it could matter). Personally, I think it's time to decide on one meaning or the other, or just retire the darn word. But until that happens, be sure to make it clear which one you mean when you use this word.

Because the company is going out of business, continuing their discussion about the best color for their logo is moot.

As his girlfriend continued to complain about his messy laundry piles during the last five minutes of the World Series, Bob wished that she would be struck mute.

more than/moreover/over

About two years ago, I learned that you shouldn't use the word *over* when you're following it with a number or fraction. Since that time, I've seen the mistake in print nearly every day. "Over 200 people came to the party." "Over half off!" "He made over $70,000 last year." Wrong, wrong, and wrong. Each of those *overs* should be replaced with a *more than*. *Over* is used when you're referring to a distance above something: "Hang the clock on the wall over the refrigerator." The same rule applies with *less than* and *under*. However, you may notice that *over* is followed by a number in magazines and newspapers, because in journalism, it's considered acceptable to save space by using *over* rather than the longer *more than*. Just because it's done this way, though, doesn't make it right. *Moreover* means further or in addition.

Since she found out her philandering husband was allergic to fish, Marcie has collected more than 150 recipes for cookies using seafood.

The Old Woman Who Lived in a Shoe decided to go to a family planning clinic; moreover, she told her husband they'd at least have to move into a boot.

That lewd comment went right over my grandmother's head.

muckraker
Please don't use this word to describe tabloid news reporters (and I use that term generously) or daytime television hosts. The original *muckrakers* were writers and critics in the early 1900s who exposed corruption in business and government.

The term *muckrake* was coined by Theodore Roosevelt in a 1906 speech; incidentally, he meant it in a derogatory way then (he didn't approve of their practices and found them to be sensationalist), although it is now widely accepted that these people—such as Ida Tarbell and Upton Sinclair—were important social reformers. Whether or not you are a fan of the original muckrakers, their goals were worthy—quite unlike the checkout-line rags that seek to expose Mel Gibson's foot fetish.

Muckraker Ida Tarbell was a leading journalist who uncovered unfair business practices.

murder *see* **assassination**

mute *see* **moot**

myriad

You never need an *of* after the word *myriad*. Don't let anyone tell you it's wrong—it isn't *wrong* per se, just unnecessary. *Myriad* can be used as a noun (meaning an immense or infinite number) or an adjective (meaning incalculable), so both of the following sentences are correct:

Myriad raindrops keep falling on my head.

A myriad of raindrops keep falling on my head.

myself

Lately, I've been hearing sentences like this: "Bob, Dave, and myself are going out to eat," and "It's important to him and myself." To the people who do this: Where are your inner gongs? Can't you hear the loud bonging noise that should be erupting in your head when you utter a sentence like this? If you can replace the word *myself* with *I* or *me*, do it. "Bob, Dave, and I are going out to eat" and "It's important to him and me" are correct. And while we're on the subject, have you ever thought about how weird the expression "I was by myself" is? You were near yourself? I'm not suggesting that you erase it from your vocabulary; just that you humor me by pondering it for a moment.

I fixed myself a salami sandwich with pickles; it's a good thing no one was eating with me.

Nn

nadir/zenith

The *zenith* is the high point; the pinnacle. If you look straight up into the sky, the point you see is also called a *zenith*. Its antonym is *nadir* (pronounced nay'-dir), which is the point in the celestial sphere that's opposite of the zenith. Likewise, nadir can be used to mean the low point; the worst part.

My life reached its zenith when my son was born.

The nadir of my year was the day I got fired, my boyfriend left me, and I got hit by a bus.

nascent/nescient

Nascent is a handy little word. It refers to something that's young but expected to grow, as in a new company or organization. *Nescient* means ignorant, or not professing belief or disbelief in God.

In 1998, we were a nascent company with only three employees; now we have thirty-three.

The nescient young woman said she would believe in God if she could see him.

nauseated/nauseous
Bet you had no idea you were using the word *nauseous* wrong! Don't worry—most of the English-speaking world misuses this word. It actually means sickening, disgusting, or gross. Something that is nauseous *causes* nausea. *Nauseous* doesn't mean you're afflicted with nausea; the correct word for that is *nauseated*.

When I cleaned out the refrigerator, I found a nauseous tuna casserole that should have been thrown out last month. Smelling it made me nauseated.

neither *see* **either**

nescient *see* **nascent**

net *see* **gross**

noisome
Noisome doesn't mean noisy. It means terribly offensive or disgusting and is usually used to describe smells.

I finally found the eight-week-old lost Easter egg by following its noisome stench to the potted plant.

nonfiction *see* fiction

nonplussed

Nonplussed doesn't mean you're unaffected or not moved; it means you're not sure how to react—you're so bewildered or shocked that you can't find the words to reply. That doesn't stop the media from getting it wrong, mind you. There have been countless reports of people who "looked nonplussed" as a verdict was read in court (meant to mean unaffected). Oh, and there's no such thing as being *plussed*, in case you were wondering.

I was nonplussed when my fiancé announced he was going to become a priest; it took me several minutes just to say "huh?"

nor

You just can't separate *nor* and *neither;* they're very close bed-fellows. "The socks are not dirty nor smelly" is incorrect. You must say, "The socks are neither dirty nor smelly."

I am neither excited nor upset about the fact that Alice and Kevin broke up; I just want to get back the waffle iron they borrowed.

notorious *see* infamous

nuclear

I would be hard-pressed to tell you anything that bothers me more than when President George W. Bush talks about "nucular war." The man whose finger is on the trigger doesn't know how to pronounce this key word, and I think his advisors are afraid to correct him. The word is *nuclear*, and it's pronounced noo-klee-ar. Is that so hard?

Nuclear wars are bad for our health.

number *see* **amount**

Oo

obfuscate

To *obfuscate* is to make something obscure or hard to understand. And you know what's so bad about these obfuscators? They usually do it on purpose.

She obfuscated the facts about the car accident, maybe to conceal that she was applying eyeliner while driving.

oblique

A little like *obfuscate*, something that is *oblique* may not be easy to understand. That's because it's misleading or not straightforward. *Oblique* also means slanted, or having a common ancestor but being related indirectly.

He made several oblique references to my finances, asking if I used coupons and shopped in thrift stores.

obsequious

Obsequious means two things: to act in a brown-nosing manner, or to be obedient to a fault; kowtowing to authority.

Of course she got an "A"—did you see how obsequious she was to the teacher, bringing him a Twinkie every day?

obtuse

How many times have you heard *obtuse* used as another word for *obscure*? ("That was an obtuse point.") Alas, no. *Obtuse* means dense (stupid), slow to understand, or displaying these qualities. In math, it also describes an angle between 90 and 180 degrees.

Maybe I'm obtuse, but I still don't understand how to program my VCR.

obviate

Nope, *obviate* doesn't mean to make something obvious—although, now that I think about it, that might be a handy word to have. But *obviate* isn't it. *Obviate* means to stop (something) from happening, or to avert a problem by staving it off at the onset.

Not serving alcohol at the wedding will obviate the bride's concern about her uncle getting drunk and embarrassing her.

odds/probability

Let's say you have a deck of fifty-two cards. You want to pick the Queen of Hearts. You can now calculate the *probability* or the *odds* that you will do so. The *probability* is a fraction that represents good outcomes/all outcomes. You have a 1/52 probability of picking the Queen of Hearts. To calculate the *odds*, you'll find the ratio of bad outcomes to good outcomes. In this case, there are 51 bad outcomes and only one good outcome, so your odds are 51:1.

The probability that your child will be a girl is 1/2 .

The odds of the Italian Stallion winning the race are 4:1.

odor *see* **aroma**

officious

Officious means overestimating your welcome; butting in where you don't belong; becoming a nuisance with your uncalled-for advice.

My officious cousin keeps telling me I need to start a retirement fund—not that I asked him for his financial advice.

older *see* **elder**

ombudsman

Ombudsmen may be employed by the legislative branch of the government to investigate complaints from people who feel that government agencies, departments, or officials have treated them unfairly. You'll also hear about *ombudsmen* in the business world—particularly in the newspaper industry. They are meant to be impartial dispute resolvers who can help to investigate claims and find solutions. Patrick Shannahan, Arizona ombudsman, says that there are five states in the United States that have classical ombudsman offices: Hawaii, Alaska, Iowa, Nebraska, and Arizona. "However, many states have ombudsmen with a jurisdiction that encompasses one agency," he says. "For example, every state has a long term care ombudsman office that helps residents of long term care facilities resolve problems." Jeffrey A. Dvorkin, ombudsman at National Public Radio, says, "A news ombudsman acts as the 'porous membrane' that allows the public to critique the news coverage. An ombudsman's ideal goal should be to find that balance which allows for journalistic accountability while raising the level of media literacy and criticism from the public."

My neighbor had trouble with a city building inspector until she called the ombudsman's office.

omnipotent/omniscient
Omnipotent is all-powerful. *Omniscient* is all-knowing. God is often described as both.

Our boss acts so omnipotent around the office that we're all a little sick of him.

In my new novel, the omniscient narrator tells the reader what's on all of the characters' minds.

optimal/optimum

Both *optimal* and *optimum* mean the best, the most positive. Be careful not to use these words as a substitute for *good*.

We had optimal conditions for the marathon today: sunny, 65 degrees, and dry.

The optimum temperature for culturing homemade yogurt is 110 degrees Fahrenheit.

option *see* choice

oral/verbal

Here's another surprise: *Verbal* and *oral* are not synonymous. *Verbal* encompasses both spoken and written words. *Oral* just deals with spoken words. If you say, "We have a verbal contract," you could be referring to either a spoken or written contract.

During Suzie's oral presentation on manners, her class-mate Tommy let out a loud belch.

In your school report, please verbalize what you did on your summer vacation.

orient/orientate

Ick. *Orientate* was never meant to be a word. "This malapropism has been used by English-depraved—just kidding—'deprived' students ('Brad is sexually orientated toward males') right up to government spokespersons at press conferences ('We must orientate ourselves to the situation'). Shudder the thought," says writer Karl Miller. The verb form of *orientation* is *orient*.

I'm still getting oriented to my new town, though I have located the doughnut shop.

ostensible
Something is *ostensible* if its appearance does not necessarily represent the truth. For example, if you drop out of school because you're being bullied, but you tell people that the reason you dropped out was because classes were too hard, then your *ostensible* reason is that classes were too hard.

Although he was ostensibly poor, he managed to buy himself a fancy new car.

ought
Ought has only one form and can't take an auxiliary verb. Therefore, "had ought to" is wrong.

We ought to have gone to the party instead of staying home and eating all the cookies.

over *see* more than

overexaggerate
To *exaggerate* is to make something sound like more than it is. So what's *overexaggerating*? I'll give you a clue: It's not a word.

And for good reason—it's unnecessary. *Exaggerate* is a strong enough word by itself.

He exaggerated his credentials when he applied for this job. He had actually never been the president of Microsoft.

overheard

The funny thing is that you probably know the definition of this word perfectly well. To *overhear* is to hear something that the speaker didn't intend for you to hear. So, then, why do people talk about *overhearing* something on television or the radio? You're darn skippy that television and radio hosts and guests fully plan for you to hear what they say. In fact, it thrills them to no end. So if you hear it in the media, then you've simply heard it, not overheard it.

I overheard Iris telling Kevin that Betty's cousin's gardener's daughter's next-door neighbor is a hussy.

overmuch

Overmuch means too much, or more than is needed.

I think I've slept overmuch; the flowers my grandmother embroidered on my pillow have made indents on my face.

Pp

paesano

We've borrowed this word from Italy. However, we're using it wrong. Most people think it means *friend*. It doesn't. That's *amico*. *Paesano* means neighbor or fellow villager.

According to the SicilianCulture.com Web site, "If you commute to work in New York City from a small New Jersey or Long Island suburb, and you see someone from the same town on the bus or train, you can say, 'Ciao, paesano.'"

My paesano John lent me his wheelbarrow.

papoose

"A lot of people think a *papoose* is the sling that the American Indians carry the baby in. It's not the sling—it's the baby," says writer Tim Mattson. Wow, who knew?

The Native American mother wrapped her papoose in a blanket.

parable *see* **allegory**

paradigm

A *paradigm* is a model or example, or a set of characteristics and beliefs shared by those in a particular field or group—for example, *the parapsychology paradigm*. Some grammarians oppose the use of the word *paradigm* to mean the popular perspective, as in "the new paradigm in cancer treatment." To be safe, avoid using it this way.

He is a paradigm of healthful living: He exercises, gets enough sleep, eats balanced meals, and doesn't smoke or drink.

paragon

A *paragon* exemplifies superiority or perfection, or is an equal. As a verb, *paragon* means to compete with, compare with, or serve as a model.

We always held up our Scrabble club president as a paragon of virtue until we found out she'd been smuggling in extra tiles.

parameter/perimeter

Parameters are established limits. *Perimeter* is the border around something, usually land.

Please stay within the parameters of good taste when you plan his bachelor party.

We have a fence running around three-quarters of the perimeter of our property.

paranoia

Unless your fears and phobias are illogical, you're not *paranoid*. Writer Linda M. Gigliotti says, "Paranoia is a rare mental disorder which includes convictions of persecution. Note the terms 'rare' and 'convictions.' Walking your eight-year-old to school so s/he doesn't come to harm, rechecking the dead bolt before you go to bed, and looking around you every few minutes on a dark and dangerous street are not paranoia. Such actions are necessary to maintain the safety you already have. Note the terms 'safety' and 'have.'"

The paranoid schizophrenic thought the KGB was spying on him through microphones implanted in his dental fillings.

paraplegic *see* **hemiplegic**

partially/partly

Someone needs to inform the weathercasters of the world that a sky can't be *partly* sunny. *Partly* implies that there's a distinguishable part; you can say that an apple is partly eaten because you can readily identify which part you ate and which part is left uneaten. A sky, however, can't be divided into parts—it doesn't have distinct boundaries. (Could you tell me which parts are sunny and which parts aren't?) Therefore, the word to use is *partially*, which means not completely; only somewhat.

People at the hospital were partially sympathetic and partially puzzled that Arthur could confuse a beer keg with a scuba tank.

The room was partly painted orange and partly covered in green striped wallpaper.

passed/past

The opposite of *future* is *past*. *Past* is a noun ("it happened in the past") or an adjective ("she is the past president of the organization"). *Passed* is a verb—it's the past tense of *pass*.

I have not eaten any doughnuts in the past three days, although I admit I drove by the shop eighteen times just to sniff.

The speeding car passed us on the highway, and then I noticed her "Grandma on Board" bumper sticker.

peak/peek/pique

A mountain has a *peak*, *peak* performance is top performance, and the *peak* hours are the busiest ones. You sneak a *peek* at something. And you try to *pique* someone's interest. If you're feeling *piqued*, your ego has been trampled and you're mad about it.

We took a chair lift to the mountain's peak, but I didn't know how to ski, so I slid all the way down on my bum.

I took a peek at my boyfriend while he was sleeping and was horrified to find his hair in curlers.

Josh was piqued when he found out he hadn't been invited to Sara's wedding.

peccadillo

Your *peccadilloes* are your little faults or transgressions.

Her tendency to leave the cap off the toothpaste after she's used it is one of her peccadilloes.

pejorative

Words or phrases can be *pejorative* if they're demeaning, insulting, or derogatory. *Pejorative* is a noun and an adjective.

"Simple" can be a pejorative word.

penultimate

Screenwriter Betsy Morris says that people think *penultimate* means "really ultimate." Lauren Teton, vice president of Name One!, adds that people sometimes think it means last. Well, guess what? It means second to last.

Irma is always the penultimate person to leave the party, because she knows that the very last person to leave is usually expected to help the host clean.

people *see* persons

percent/percentage

If you're using a number, you can follow it with *percent*. When no number is involved, the appropriate word is *percentage*.

Forty percent of women are more afraid of trying on a bikini than of getting mugged.

A large percentage of lottery winners promise to donate their winnings to charity.

peremptory/preemptory
Peremptory is not related to preempt. The adjective form of preempt is "preemptive." *Peremptory* means commanding, not open to debate, or authoritative. *Preemptory* is a word you'll probably never use; it means "relating to a settler's right to buy public land at a fixed price."

Father gave us a peremptory order to clean our rooms before we went to bed, so we pooled our allowance money and called Dial-A-Maid.

perennial *see* **annual**

perimeter *see* **parameter**

pernicious
If something is *pernicious*, it has a detrimental effect or influence.

Being around depressed people has had a pernicious effect on the company psychologist's mood, so management moved her to a windowless office on the ground floor for her own safety.

personable/personal

A person can be *personable* if he or she is congenial and/or attractive. Inanimate objects can't be personable, even though I've seen *personable* used to describe pictures, machines, and computer programs today. (*Personable* doesn't mean having human characteristics.) Something that is *personal* is private, particular to a person, or concerning a person's body.

Jane is so personable that every convenience store clerk in the county knows her by name.

I don't want to tell you my salary; that's personal.

persons/people

Ugh. The *persons* people are just pompous twits. There is no good reason to use the word *persons*. The plural of *person* is *people*. To be really generous to the opposing team here, I'll tell you that *persons* can be used similarly to *bodies*, although I still hate it. If someone asks, "Do they have any weapons on their persons?" that means "Are they carrying, wearing, or keeping weapons anywhere in or on their bodies?" But never ask, "How many persons are coming?" That's just silly.

Many people on my block still had their Christmas lights up in March.

perspective/prospective

It's *prospective* that gets mangled into *perspective* sometimes.

pe...

When you put something in *perspective*, you consider it in relation to a bigger picture—you don't blow it out of proportion. *Perspective* also means a view (physical or mental). *Prospective* means possible in the future, or likely to become.

What's your perspective on the issue of salsa dancing lessons in the nursing home?

Right now we're just dating casually, and until I check his credit rating, he's just my prospective boyfriend.

perspicacity

Perspicacity is the ability to size up a situation quickly and come to correct conclusions; to grasp things without much explanation, or to have accurate intuition. Its adjective is *perspicacious*.

Because of his perspicacity, my six-year-old was able to learn the computer program and explain it to me in just an hour.

persuade *see* **convince**

pertinence *see* **impertinence**

peruse

Okay, this one shocked me. *Peruse* doesn't mean to skim—actually, it means precisely the opposite. It means to study carefully. If I were a betting woman, I'd put money on the odds that popular usage will eventually cause this accepted definition to change.

Please peruse the pressure cooker's how-to manual before you call the fire department to take off the lid.

picayune
Picayune means petty, or of little significance or value; trivial. It likely comes from the French word *picaillon*, which means a five-cent coin.

When I realized how much she was suffering from falling into the cactus, my own complaint of chipping a fingernail seemed picayune.

pique *see* peak

pithy
I always thought this meant something like *flaky*, so when a friend of mine asked me for a *pithy* quote, I was offended. But, no! My friend was asking for a succinct, clever quote: something that gets across its meaning in few words.

The governor's pithy comments made it clear that he—or at least his speechwriter—was opposed to the death penalty.

pitted
My sister says she always has to think twice when she sees the words *pitted olives;* does that mean they have pits or they don't have pits? Turns out it means they don't. Something is

pitted if the pits have been removed.

    Even though the package said the prunes were pitted, Jasper broke two front teeth when he chomped down on a big pit.

plan
Don't *plan on* anything. That's incorrect grammar. Just plan it, or plan to, or plan for.

    We planned to go to Disney World but ended up in the transmission repair shop.

plethora
A *plethora* is an excess. It doesn't just mean "many." If you have a plethora of options, you don't just have several options—you have too many options.

    So many guests brought cakes and cookies to our neighborhood Thanksgiving potluck dinner that we had a plethora of desserts; too bad nobody thought to bake a turkey.

plurality *see* majority

pneumoultramicroscopicsilicovolcanoconiosis
Yes, fine, I did throw this one in just for fun. I just get annoyed when people tell me *antidisestablishmentarianism* is the longest English word. According to my dictionary, it's *pneumoultramicroscopicsilicovolcanoconiosis*, a disease of the lungs

caused by inhaling volcanic dust. I did a science report on this disease in the fourth grade; I wonder if that tells you precisely how much of a nerd I am.

podium *see* **lectern**

pontificate

When people say, "I'm just pontificating," what they usually mean to say is "I'm just guessing." Little do they know that what they're really saying is, "I'm just being a pompous, arrogant jerk." To *pontificate* is to express your opinion like a know-it-all. In the Roman Catholic religion, *pontificate* also means to do the job of a pontiff—the pope.

The assistant interim public defender's law clerk pontificated about the court case as if he were the judge.

pool *see* **billiards**

populace/populous

The *populace* is the public. *Populous* means highly populated.

The politician lost the populace's respect when he got caught shoplifting at an adult video store.

Manhattan is a populous island; it's home to more than 1,500,000 people.

po:

popular

Funny thing about *popular*—most people know it means well-liked or generally accepted, and yet, it's often used wrong. When kids talk scornfully about the *popular* kids at their school, they're often referring to the snooty kids who most of the other kids *don't* like. And you should never use the word *popular* when you're describing something negative—for example, "Driver intoxication is the most popular cause of fatal car accidents" is wrong. (Is it really the most well-liked cause?) Instead, say it's the most common cause.

Knitting is a popular pastime of elderly women, and lately, of Hollywood stars on movie sets.

pore/pour

According to an Associated Press headline, Maryland police *poured* over shooting data. You can't *pour over* something . . . well, unless you're spilling a liquid over it. What that editor meant was *pore*. To *pore* is to read thoroughly, to stare, or to carefully consider. *Pores* are also those tiny holes in your skin that have inspired eight gazillion expensive cleaning products.

The police pored over the evidence to try to crack the case of the missing beaver.

Please pour me a glass of eggnog.

port *see* bow

postmodernist

While I was visiting my cousin in San Francisco, she kept referring to a group of her artsy friends as the "postmodernist boys."
I did a good deal of head-scratching, wondering how someone
who is alive right now could be an after-modern person. Turns
out that *modernism* was a movement that followed the Victo-
rian era, wherein artists, musicians, and writers rejected Victo-
rian standards and created new art. A lot of the work created
during this time (the late nineteenth century through the twen-
tieth century) included stream-of-consciousness writing; work
that defied genre boundaries; and art techniques such as
impressionism, collages, and minimalism.

"Postmodernism, like modernism, follows most of these
same ideas . . . [favoring] reflexivity and self-consciousness, fragmentation and discontinuity (especially in narrative structures),
ambiguity, simultaneity, and an emphasis on the destructured,
decentered, dehumanized subject," says Dr. Mary Klages, asso-
ciate professor, English Department, University of Colorado,
Boulder, in her article "Postmodernism" (December 3, 1997) on
the University of Colorado Web site (*www.colorado.edu*).

"But—while postmodernism seems very much like modernism in these ways, it differs from modernism in its attitude
toward a lot of these trends . . . Many modernist works try to
uphold the idea that works of art can provide the unity, coher-
ence, and meaning [that] has been lost in most of modern life;

art will do what other human institutions fail to do. Postmodernism, in contrast, doesn't lament the idea of fragmentation, provisionality, or incoherence, but rather celebrates that. The world is meaningless? Let's not pretend that art can make meaning then, let's just play with nonsense."

potable
As an adjective, *potable* means appropriate for drinking. As a noun, it means a drink, especially an alcoholic one.
   Shall we imbibe potables this evening?

pour *see* **pore**

pray/prey
When you're talking to God or begging someone, you're *praying*. An animal that is eaten is the *prey* of another animal. People and things can be *prey* if they're vulnerable to attack or likely to be harmed. If you *prey* on someone, you're taking advantage of him or her. That person has *fallen prey* to you.
   The Miss America candidate said she prayed for world peace.
   Once Henry flashed his platinum credit card, he was easy prey for the tropical fish salesmen.

precede/proceed
To *precede* is to come or happen before: Monday precedes

Tuesday. The president *precedes* the vice president because the president's rank comes before the vice president's. To *proceed* is to continue or to start.

Lightning preceded the thunder.

We are proceeding with the surprise party for Grandpa's ninety-eighth birthday tomorrow, even though Grandma blabbed, because he won't remember anyway.

preemptory *see* **peremptory**

preplanning
Planning is, by the definition of the word, done in advance. So why would you ever need the prefix *pre-*? You wouldn't, no matter what the funeral industry says. *Pre-* means prior, so you're just needlessly repeating yourself by using the word *preplanning*.

presently
I am well aware that this meaning is odd, but *presently* doesn't mean now. It means soon. If you mean that something is happening now, say it's happening *currently*.

I will presently graduate from the correspondence school of brain surgery.

presume *see* **assume**

pr...

prevaricate

To *prevaricate* is to act evasively, or to avoid telling the truth by being vague in your statements.

She prevaricated when we asked where she was last night, saying that she was "just driving around."

prevent

"'The brake is used to prevent the car from going through the red light.' Well, everyone knows you don't *prevent* something from doing something. You *prevent* something, period," says Graeme McRae (*http://mcraeclan.com/graeme/Language/*). "So what do you prevent by using the brake? You might be tempted to say the thing you prevent is 'the car going through the red light.' But that makes it seem like you're preventing the car while the car happens to be going through the red light. To make it clear you're preventing the going and not the car you could say you're preventing the 'car's going through the red light.' By using the possessive you make 'going' the only possible thing to be prevented."

I prevented a catastrophe by seating the man and his ex-wife on opposite sides of the room.

preventative/preventive

Because *preventative* means the same thing as *preventive*, there's no good reason to use the longer word.

I'm taking preventive measures to avoid getting my heart broken again: I've quit dating and am becoming a nun.

prey *see* **pray**

principle/principal

Your *principles* are your morals. *Principles* are also ideas (as in, "according to communist principles . . ."). If you understand something *in principle*, it means you understand the idea behind it, but you may not understand how it's practiced. The *principal* is someone who is in charge, particularly the head of a school. It can also refer to someone who has an important role (the *principals* in the strike negotiations), or a sum of money. In acting, a *principal* is someone with a speaking part. Also, *principal* can be used as an adjective, meaning main or primary.

My principles won't allow me to shoplift, no matter how much I want that matching pair of orange bowling balls.

The principal reason for the new law is to ensure that people who sing off-key in church will be properly reprimanded.

priority

A *priority* can be high or low, so if you say something is *a priority*, you're not actually saying that it's very important. Your *priorities* are things that you want to accomplish, but a particular

pr...

priority can fall anywhere on the list, so you may want to clarify by saying something is a *high priority*.

> *Making enough money to buy doughnuts is a high priority in my life.*

prison *see* jail

pristine
If something is *pristine*, it's not just sparkling clean—it's in its original (new) condition. While the kitchen floor might be spotless, it's not *pristine* unless it looks just like it did when you first bought it.

> *For sale: pristine exercise equipment, never used.*

probability *see* odds

proceed *see* precede

prodigal
Writer Marli Murphy's book club read Barbara Kingsolver's *Prodigal Summer*, and one of the members said she couldn't figure out how the title related to the book after she'd read it. Like Murphy, the other members had always thought the word meant favored or chosen, because of the Bible story of the prodigal son. Many people also believe it has something to do

with being gone for a long time and then returning home. Wrong! It actually means wasteful, given to excess, or plentiful. Murphy says, "One of our members who is more religious than the rest of us explained that in the Bible story, the prodigal son is reckless and wasteful and given to excess, but when he repents, he is warmly welcomed home by his family. *Prodigal* is what he was before he repented." (By the way, they decided it meant "plentiful" in Kingsolver's title.)

The prodigal woman has 106 pairs of shoes in four different sizes.

prone/supine
You're *prone* if you're lying on your belly, face down. You're *supine* if you're lying on your back.

I always sleep in a prone position because I don't want bedbugs to crawl into my navel.

Gary was supine on the beach blanket when the seagull attacked his nose.

prospective *see* perspective

prosperity
You can be poor and still be *prosperous. Prosperity* merely means success; you can be successful in many ways that aren't financial, can't you?

She was a prosperous writer, having written for major magazines such as Good Housekeeping *and* Family Circle, *even though she probably would have earned more money working in a fast-food restaurant.*

prostrate/prostate

The *prostate* is the gland in males that produces the fluid part of semen. When a person is *prostrate,* she is lying face down (yes, just like *prone*), usually as a sign of kowtowing or obedience—or she's exhausted and weak.

She prostrated herself in front of the queen and noticed that the floor smelled like bleach.

Joe is worried that he might have prostate cancer.

prototype

According to *The Chapel Hill News,* "UNC Sports Clubs director Steve Bradley-Bull said those who will compete at any level regardless of the glory involved are prototypical sports club members." What he means here is that they're good examples of sports club members, or archetypal. That's not what *prototypical* means. A *prototype* is the first model of something.

My dad built a prototype of a fish bicycle to present to the patent attorney.

proved/proven

As a verb, the preferred form is *proved*. (You can say that something *was proved* or *has been proved*.) If you're using it as an adjective, the word is *proven* (a *proven solution*, a *proven alternative*).

I think he has proved that he is sorry for missing your birthday; now will you wash off his tar and feathers?

The teacher has a proven record of turning "D" students into "C-" students.

provided/providing

I often hear sentences like this: "I'll go, providing my kids can come with me." Nope. The word that belongs in place of *providing* is *provided*. Only *provided* can mean "on the condition that." *Providing* means supplying.

I'll go out to eat with you, provided you pay.

Shelly will be providing the beer for poker night.

proximity

Don't bother saying something is in *close proximity* to something else. *Proximity* already means close. There's no such thing as being in *far proximity*.

The train station is in proximity to several fast-food restaurants, and conductor Terrell has the waistline to prove it.

pr...

prurient

Prurient is lustful, or exhibiting an extreme interest in sex.

I think those magazines are igniting his prurient side.

psychic *see* **clairaudient**

pulpit *see* **lectern**

pundit

A *pundit* is someone with expertise; a guru. It can also mean a source of opinion or a critic, such as a political pundit.

Because Tom is an etiquette pundit, Edna asked him how to word an apology letter for her goat eating the neighbor's turnip greens.

Qq

quadriplegic *see* hemiplegic

quandary *see* dilemma

query *see* inquiry

quotation/quote
Quote isn't just shorthand for *quotation*. *Quote* is only a verb; it means to reiterate someone else's exact words. *Quotation* is only a noun. It refers to the words that have been quoted.

I used a quotation from Walt Whitman in my speech.

May I quote you about how much you love our new doughnut-flavored toothpaste?

Rr

rack/wrack

You *rack* your brain, and some things are nerve-*racking*. To *rack* is to torture, torment, cause ruin, or put into a rack. When you talk about *racking* your brain or your nerves, you're torturing them, as if you're stretching them out on the medieval torture device ("the rack"). If something is *wracked*, it's wrecked. You typically only see the noun *wrack* in the phrase *wrack and ruin*, which is pretty redundant anyway, since the noun *wrack* means ruin or obliteration. Just in case I haven't confused you yet, for both meanings of *wrack*, the alternate spelling is *rack*.

> *He was racked with pain after his tongue piercing.*
> *The entire wharf district was wracked after the hurricane.*

radical

The 1980s brought us the use of *radical* as a slang word for *cool* (which is a slang word itself). There's no good reason for this usage. *Radical* doesn't mean cool, nor does it mean different, unusual, or great. It means *highly* different from the norm, or wanting great social or political change. It can also mean relating to the root or core of something.

Herman might have been appointed to the mayor's Board of Culture had it not been for his radical views in favor of pig wrestling at the annual Mardi Gras ball.

raise/rear

"Almost everyone thinks they *raise* their children," says writer Carol Celeste. "Animals are *raised*, but children should be *reared*." *Raising children* is a colloquialism. Actually, animals can be *reared*, too. To *rear* is to take care of (youngsters) until they are self-sufficient.

We raise wheat, milo, and corn on our farm.

Pardon me for not having much time to socialize; I'm busy rearing three children . . . and their father.

raze

When you *raze* something, you destroy it until there is nothing left. *Razing* a building means tearing it down so it's level with the ground. Therefore, it's redundant to use the phrase *raze to the ground.*

The tornado razed the barn but left the scarecrow standing.

Realtor®

Realtor® is not a generic word for people who work in real estate. It's a trademarked term, and refers specifically to a member of the National Association of Realtors. That's why you keep seeing that annoying "®" sign.

Our Realtor® sold our house for fair market value.

rear *see* raise

rebut/refute

A reporter for the *Catholic Herald* wrote, "Jill Dryer, spokeswoman for Mercy Healthcare Sacramento, strongly refuted charges that the hospital system acted improperly." Bzzz! Sorry, wrong word. To *refute* is to disprove. What this reporter meant was *rebut*, which means to deny or argue against a claim.

Maybelle refuted the allegation that she committed the assault by showing the bill that proved she was at a motel with Sugarlips Bailey, the sheriff's deputy, at the time of the crime.

Rob rebutted Patti's accusation that he had been speaking to his ex-girlfriend.

recognizance/reconnaissance

"Former National Intelligence Agency officer and retired Lieutenant Colonel Mehmet Korkut Eken who had been released on his own reconnaissance did not attend the hearing," reported the *Turkish Daily News*. "Reeder was released on personal reconnaissance bond," reported the *York County Coast Star*. Well, smack me in the forehead. So these suspects were soldiers who were released from jail to go on a mission to spy on the enemy? Because that's what *reconnaissance* means, you know. In the unlikely event that these esteemed newspapers were wrong, then perhaps the word that has eluded them is *recognizance*, which means "an obligation of record entered into before a court or officer duly authorized for that purpose, with a condition to do some act required by law, which is therein specified," according to the 'Lectric Law Library (*www.lectlaw.com*). The act required by law is usually to appear in court. A person who is released on his or her *own recognizance* doesn't have to pay a bond.

The soldiers were sent on a reconnaissance mission in Iraq.

The district attorney, accused of having twenty-three unpaid parking tickets, was released on his own recognizance.

recur/reoccur

Reoccur isn't a standard word. Something that happens more than once *recurs*.

I have a recurring nightmare that someone has stolen all my doughnuts.

redoubtable

From the looks of this word, you might think it means the state of doubting again. But just to throw you off course, it usually means intimidating. If someone is *redoubtable*, he has a commanding presence, and people are afraid of him. *Redoubtable* can also mean worthy of admiration or deference.

In the television show The Sopranos, *Tony Soprano is a redoubtable man who strikes fear in the hearts of his daughter's suitors.*

refute *see* rebut

regime/regimen/regiment

Writer Cora Scott says, "People use *regime* (a system of rule, government, or administration) when they mean *regimen* (a regulated routine of therapy or exercise designed to promote health; any system that is in place)." A *regiment* is a military unit. As a verb, *regiment* means to command as a strong disciplinarian, or to organize into units.

The subversive group in the bingo hall wants to overthrow the current regime because of their policy against coveralls.

I follow a strict exercise regimen . . . sometimes.

The teacher regimented her "trouble" students, ordering them to shine her shoes and wear signs that said things like "I am a bed-wetter" when they misbehaved.

reign/rein

A king *reigns* (rules) over his kingdom. Happiness *reigns* in your heart. Santa Claus pulls on *reins* to control his reindeer.

The reigning Miss America expressed strong feelings about finding a cure for the common cold.

Pull on the reins if you want your horse to stop.

reiterate *see* iterate

remuneration/renumeration

There's no such word as *renumeration;* people tend to say it because it sounds like it includes *number,* but the correct word is *remuneration,* meaning compensation (usually payment). Instead of thinking "number," think "money."

I don't expect any kind of remuneration for baby sitting. By the way, that imported cheese was really good, you're out of root beer and macadamia nuts, and I used up that long-distance phone card that was in your underwear drawer.

reoccur *see* recur

repel/repulse

If someone disgusts you, you are *repelled,* not *repulsed. Repulse* means to push away or to scorn. But, yes, *repellent* and *repulsive* both mean the act of pushing away or causing disgust.

What can I say? We speak a weird language.

I am repelled by your armpit flatulence noises.

Helena repulsed George's advances, telling him she never dates men with comb-overs.

replica

You should only use the word *replica* when referring to a copy that is produced by the maker of the original. In other cases, just use the word *copy*.

Artist Kenny DeSanto made several replicas of his painting.

respectively

Respectively means "in that order." When someone says, "Greg, Margaret, and Ed got eleven, fourteen, and five votes, respectively," that means Greg got eleven votes, Margaret got fourteen, and Ed got five.

The Olivers and the Jungs have three and two kids, respectively.

résumé *see* curriculum vitae

retch/wretch

When you get the feeling that you're about to vomit, you *retch*. A *wretch* is a bad, sad, or pitiable person.

I thought I would retch when I walked into the locker room, which smelled like feet.

I would never give money to that wretch who sits on the stoop outside our building; I'd rather give him food.

reticent

Primarily, *reticent* means disinclined to speak, or preferring to keep silent, particularly about thoughts or feelings. However, it can also be used to describe a person, place, or thing that exhibits restraint in appearance or expression, or has a reserved style. I'm not thrilled about its use as a synonym for *reluctant*, but if you must, at least beware of saying that you are *reticent* to talk about something—that would be redundant.

When our marriage was rocky, my husband became reticent about his finances, switching the subject whenever I brought it up.

retrograde

If something is *retrograde*, it's moving backwards (or, in the case of astronomic bodies, at least appearing to move backwards, or in opposition to the usual rotation). *Retrograde* can also describe something that's taken a figurative step backwards; something that's gotten worse.

After the rap band moved in next door, the house's condition took a retrograde turn.

revenge *see* **avenge**

rife

If your life is *rife with* heartache, it's full of heartache. *Rife* also means commonplace or widespread.

Six days after the famous couple got married, gossip columns were rife with rumors that the couple was experiencing irreconcilable differences.

robbed/stolen

"A masked man robbed all of Simon's money." What's wrong with this sentence? Money can't be *robbed*. The object of the verb *rob* is the person from whom, or place from which, something is taken—a person or place can be *robbed*. The aforementioned sentence needs the verb *stole*, whose object is the thing that has been snatched (in this case, the money). Otherwise, it reads as if the money had something taken away from it.

Barry ran from the wig store, holding his hands over his bristly scalp and shouting, "I was robbed!"

The biology department's mascot was stolen. Now, what would somebody want with a ten-foot-tall statue of a lab rat?

robbery *see* **burglary**

Ss

salient

I don't know about you, but the only time I hear the word *salient* is in the phrase *salient points*. Nonetheless, it's good to know what it means, especially so we can encourage more diversity for this unfairly pigeonholed word. (Imagine the poor little *salient*, holding up a picket sign: "I can describe more than just points!") *Salient* means most significant, sticking out, bouncing, or jumping. Not to make fun of our country's higher education system, but an Internet search turned out dozens of assignments from professors who wanted students to outline the "most salient points" of something or other. Since *salient* already means most significant (or important), those professors are being repetitive.

For Wanda, the salient issue in her life is whether or not she'll make it home from the tavern in time to watch the new late-night infomercials.

sanguine/sanguinary

These are two mighty different words. *Sanguine* means hopeful and confident (or reddish); *sanguinary* means wanting to kill or be violent, or marked by bloodshed.

Fran is sanguine about getting her book proposal accepted; she's already bought a new outfit in case The Today Show *wants to interview her when the book becomes a bestseller.*

The sanguinary father hunted for the man who assaulted his daughter.

sank/sunk

"Have you found *sunk* used in the past perfect form?" writer Sam AJ Pillay asked me. "'The boat sunk after it was hit,' for example? In my view, *sank* would be the appropriate term, but it seems to me that this abuse has almost been accepted by the world of the lexicons." Right, Sam, but as I said, I'm not giving up on the good fight. *Sunk* is a past participle, and the correct phrase would be *the boat has sunk*.

My heart sank when I found out my daughter didn't get the part of Dorothy in the school play and will instead be playing one of the flying monkeys.

My hopes of being a dot-com millionaire were sunk after I realized that nobody wants to buy fruitcakes online.

scarf/scoff

My mom was sure she'd found a good word pair for me to include in this book. "Do you *scarf* down food or *scoff* it down?" she asked. "Even I'm not sure, and I was an English teacher." "Scarf," I answered. And I was pretty sure of myself, right until I looked it up and found out that either word can be used to mean eat like a pig. They're both slang, and they're both acceptable in informal speech or writing. To *scoff* is also to make fun of or treat with scorn.

I scarfed (scoffed) down a whole bag of chocolate chip cookies.

Sure, they're all scoffing at me now, but just wait until I get a patent on these edible shoelaces and become a millionaire.

schizophrenia

When I took a course in abnormal psychology, my professor complained about how many people think *schizophrenics* have more than one personality. There have even been movies and books that commit this error. In fact, the correct name for that disorder is multiple personality disorder (MPD). According to the *DSM-IV*, the diagnostic tool that mental health professionals use to diagnose mental illnesses, *schizophrenia* is a psychotic disorder that's marked by delusions, hallucinations, disorganized or incoherent speech, disorganized or catatonic behavior, and/or negative symptoms such as flat affect, reduced speech, or lack of volition. Evidence of the disorder must be present for at least six months, must impair the patient's life, and mood disorders must be excluded before a diagnosis of schizophrenia can be made.

Although schizophrenia only affects about one percent of the population, it is estimated that up to one-third of all homeless people in America and the United Kingdom are schizophrenic.

seasonal/seasonable

Seasonable weather is what's expected for the season. *Seasonal* means connected to the season.

My seasonal allergies always act up in spring.

Thanks to seasonable weather, everyone was comfortable without jackets during our May walk-a-thon.

seems *see* appears

segue

To *segue* (not spelled segway, although that's the way it's pronounced) is to make a smooth transition from one thing to the next. You'll hear this word a lot on late-night television talk shows—Conan O'Brien is always talking about *segueing* from one topic to the next in his interviews. *Segue* is also a noun.

This morning I wrote an article about multiple orgasms, and this afternoon I had to write an article about Social Security policy. I found it difficult to segue from one subject to the other.

semantics

"We didn't win" means the same thing as "we lost." What's the difference? *Semantics:* the way something is worded, or the interpretation of a word, phrase, or sentence. "A politician who says 'negative housing starts were up last year' is using semantics," says writer Mary J. Schirmer. "He means we aren't building as many new houses this year as we did last year."

My daughter was using semantics when she said she had been specially selected by the dean; the truth is that she had been "specially selected" for detention.

semiweekly *see* **biweekly**

sensual/sensuous

These two words have the same denotation: pleasing to, relating to, or stimulating the senses. They differ slightly in connotation, though: *Sensual* is more often used to describe something sexual, or apply to the sense of touch, whereas *sensuous* is used to apply to any of the senses, and doesn't have to carry a sexual overtone.

He gave her a sensual foot rub.
The sensuous aroma of apple pie filled the air.

set/sit

Set is usually a transitive verb, which means it requires a direct object. *Sit* is usually intransitive. You *set* something down; you don't *sit* it down. Exceptions: the sun sets, things (like senility) can set in, and you can sit yourself down.

> *Before he proposed, the millionaire set a prenuptial agreement on the table.*

> *The cat sat on my hat and got hair all over it.*

several *see* **couple**

sewn/sown
Unless you're doing it with a needle and thread (which would require a tremendous amount of patience), you're not *sewing* any seeds. Seeds are *sown* (planted). So are wild oats.

> *Aunt Hilda thought little Bobby's underwear were all ripped, and he found that she had sewn shut all the flies.*

> *I thought you would have sown your wild oats by the time you were thirty.*

sex *see* **gender**

shear/sheer
You usually hear about *shearing* in terms of sheep—meaning that they have their wool shaved off. But a person can be *shorn*, too, when he (or she) gets a "buzz-cut." Anything you cut with shears is *shorn*. *Shear* can be used figuratively, too—if someone is *shorn of* her duties, it means that her

duties have been stripped away from her. See-through fabric is *sheer*.

The farmer sheared his sheep, which caused the family's cocker spaniel to hide for three days.

Those sheer drapes aren't going to block out any light.

sherbet/sorbet

Sherbet (which has no second "r") has milk in it, and *sorbet* does not. They're both frozen desserts made from sugar (or other sweeteners), fruit juices, fruit flavorings, and stabilizer. *Sherbet* is a cross between *sorbet* and ice cream.

There's nothing like sherbet on a summer day.

Because I'm lactose-intolerant, I prefer sorbet.

shock *see* electrocute

sight *see* cite

simile *see* metaphor

since *see* ago *and* because

sit *see* set

site *see* cite

size

Size isn't an adjective. Never. It's a noun and a verb. So avoid saying, "Any size dog will need training." Say, "A dog of any size will need training."

I wonder how many women are telling the truth when they say size doesn't matter; I prefer a small heel.

slander *see* **defamation**

sleight/slight

You're likely to see *sleight* only in the magician's phrase *sleight of hand*. A *sleight* is a trick, or adroitness. All of the other meanings are meant for *slight*. *Slight* means slender and dainty, or very little in amount or degree. If you feel slighted, you feel overlooked.

Using sleight of hand, he made the slight woman disappear.

sneaked

The past tense of *sneak* is *sneaked*. *Snuck* is colloquial.

We sneaked past the guard and got free admission to the Bible Conference.

sorbet *see* **sherbet**

sown *see* **sewn**

starboard *see* bow

stationary/stationery
If something is *stationary*, it's standing still. *Stationery* is the stuff you write on.
> *Please stay stationary; I'm trying to draw your picture.*
> *True writers always have too much stationery.*

stern *see* bow

stolen *see* robbed

stopgap
I had heard the word *stopgap* many times on CNN before I bothered to find out what it meant. When someone talks about taking *stopgap measures* to solve a problem, it means he's using a "Band-Aid" solution: creating a quick fix on the fly to deal with the problem for the time being. *Stopgap* is also a noun.
> *Duct tape around the leaky tailpipe was a successful stopgap until Dexter could save up for a new exhaust system.*

strident
A *strident* sound is one that is loud and abrasive. It's not just loud; it has to be annoying.

The child's strident screams for more peanuts rang out through the airplane.

sublime

For the longest time, I thought *sublime* meant "subtle" because of the way it's often used to describe nuances in music and art-work. It actually means very pleasing, remarkable, noble, or highly worthy.

The most sublime view Mary has ever seen was from the top of Engineer's Pass in Colorado, where she was standing higher than clouds and looking down at mountaintops.

sunk *see* sank

superego *see* ego

supernova

According to NASA, a *supernova* is "the death explosion of a massive star, resulting in a sharp increase in brightness fol-lowed by a gradual fading. At peak light output, supernova explosions can outshine a galaxy. The outer layers of the exploding star are blasted out in a radioactive cloud. This expanding cloud, visible long after the initial explosion fades from view, forms a supernova remnant (SNR)."

In February of 1987, a supernova in the Large Magellanic

Cloud became visible to those in the Southern Hemisphere.

supine *see* **prone**

supplant/supplement
One dear writing friend of mine told me that he *supplants* his usual writing income with public relations work. I didn't have the heart to tell him that *supplant* means to replace. (I just decided to humiliate him publicly instead; how kind of me. At least I left out his name.) The word he should have used was *supplement*, which means to bolster or add to. In math, *supplementary angles* are made up of two angles that add up to 180 degrees.

I think DVDs are slowly supplanting videos.

The store owner supplements his business by working as Barney at children's birthday parties.

sycophantic/unctuous
Someone who is *sycophantic* fawns over powerful people. *Unctuous* doesn't have to apply to people in authority; you can be unctuous to anyone. It means fake niceness, describing someone who puts on a false front to gain someone's favor.

The sycophantic intern complimented the boss on his floral polyester pants.

Your sister is so unctuous toward me; I know she says nasty things behind my back.

symbiosis

I overuse this word the way some people overuse *pro-active*. That's just because I really like it. In its literal sense, *symbiosis* means living together, and is used to describe organisms of different species that live in close associations and are codependent (for example, birds that eat the ticks off rhinoceroses), or in some cases, in a parasitic relationship. In its extended sense (the one I like so much), *symbiosis* is a relationship that occurs when both parties depend on and benefit from each other.

I have a symbiotic relationship with my editor; I write whatever she needs to fill the next issue, and she writes the checks that pay my bills.

sympathize *see* empathize

syndrome *see* disease

synergy

Synergy occurs when two or more factors work in conjunction for a positive outcome. The combined result is stronger than the individual results.

EBay and PayPal have combined forces and have found a terrific working synergy.

Tt

taciturn

Similar to *reticent*, this word means habitually disinclined to talk; disliking conversation; a man of few words.

Sally tried to find out the secret of how Billy Bob learned to levitate, but he's a taciturn man who uttered only, "Read my book, Levitation for Morons.*"*

take *see* **bring**

tapestry

A *tapestry* is not just any wall hanging, although it's come to be used that way, just like Kleenex® has come to mean any tissue even though it's a brand name. (I hope this counts as product placement, because I could use some free tissues. Maybe I should also mention Mercedes-Benz.) A *tapestry* is made of a thick cloth with a hand-woven, usually multicolored pictorial design. Figuratively, *tapestry* can be used to mean something of complicated design.

My career has been a tapestry of imagination, success, failure, and euphoria.

taunt/taut

You can't hold something *taunt*. Holding it *taut* is perfectly acceptable, though, as long as you mean to hold it tightly stretched out. When you *taunt* someone, you tease, torture, or mock him.

Hold the material taut so I can finish sewing it.

The bully taunted Poindexter, the boy who was chosen last for the soccer team in gym class. Years later, Poindexter owned a multimillion-dollar computer company, where the bully worked as a custodian.

tautology

You're guilty of *tautology* if you pointlessly repeat yourself using different words. And a *tautology* has been made if you say the same thing in a different way. (Uh . . . just joking!)

It was a tautology when Jim said, "I was in so much pain and it really hurt!"

tee shirt *see* T-shirt

teem

To *teem* is to be full of, especially used to describe something that's bustling with activity, or swarming.

During the last full-moon ceremony, the sand around the campfire was teeming with fire ants, and Warrior Who Wears Sandals has the welts to prove it.

telekinetic *or* telepathic *see* clairaudient

temperature *see* fever

tenant/tenet
Tenants are those poor souls who work overtime just so they can pay their landlords on the first of every month. *Tenets* are beliefs, principles, or rules held by individuals or groups. I hear that landlords have no tenets.

I was a tenant in an apartment in Boston before the building was condemned.

According to the tenets of the Catholic church, abortion is immoral.

tenderhooks/tenterhooks
There's no such standard word as *tenderhooks*. *Tenterhooks*, however, is a perfectly good word. As Joan Morris explains in the Contra Costa *Times*, "When a weaver finishes weaving a piece of cloth, it is stretched tight on a frame called a *tenter*. *Tenterhooks* are what hold the fabric taut. Therefore, if someone is *on tenterhooks*, they are in a state of great tension and suspense."

Don't keep me on tenterhooks—tell me who got voted off the island on Survivor!

terrific

Ever heard someone talk about his or her "terrific troubles" or "a terrific car accident," and thought, "What a weirdo"? *Terrific* doesn't always mean great; in fact, its first meaning is "terrifying." It can also mean lousy or astonishing.

I heard a terrific crashing noise and ran to my infant's room to make sure she was okay.

than/then

When you're making a comparison, the proper word is *than* ("She is smarter than I am"). When you're referring to time, or you mean "also" or "in that case," the proper word is *then* ("We'll go to the movies, then we'll grab a bite to eat"). I don't often see people substituting the word *than* for *then*, but I see the reverse quite often—such as "She is smarter then I am." (Well, maybe she is!)

The Johnsons are friendlier than the Smiths.

I'll pay my credit card bill, and then I'll eat ramen noodles for three weeks.

thanks

Have you ever noticed *thanks to* when gratitude is totally inappropriate? "Thanks to a cruel boss, Terrie was forced to work on

Christmas Eve." ("Thanks, cruel boss!") Don't give thanks where thanks aren't due. That sentence could be reworked a few ways: "Terrie was forced to work on Christmas Eve because she had a cruel boss" or "Terrie's cruel boss made her work on Christmas Eve" both work just fine, without the unnecessary thankfulness.

Thanks to TV dinners, I may never have to cook again.

that/which

Wait, that wasn't your last lesson on *that*. There's also the *that/which* distinction, which confuses a lot of people. "It seems to me just plain obvious that *which* describes the members of a class while *that* restricts the membership of a class," says Graeme McRae (*http://mcraeclan.com/graeme/Language/*). "Example: 'The computers, which have DVD players, need frequent rebooting,' or 'The computers that have DVD players need frequent rebooting.' The first uses *which* to describe the computers. The second uses *that* to restrict the class under consideration to just those computers that have DVD players, implying that DVD players somehow contribute to the computers' instability." If it's part of an essential clause (that is, the meaning of the sentence would be changed without it), use *that*. If it's a nonessential clause, use *which*. A quick and dirty rule is that *which* generally follows a comma, whereas *that* doesn't.

The doughnuts that have coconut topping are my favorites.

The shoe polish they call coffee, which I bought at the gas station, could take the paint off my car.

that/who

"TV newscasters, print reporters, ad copywriters, politicians, esteemed colleagues—lots of people seem to be using *that* as the all-purpose word," says Cynthia Amorese, and I couldn't agree more. Never use *that* when you're referring to a person. For example, "the man that walked me home" and "the girl that left her pocketbook on the train" are both wrong. People always get *who* ("the man who walked me home" and "the girl who left her pocketbook on the train"). Places and things get *that* ("the restaurant that serves the best steak" and "the sweater that I wear every time I go skiing").

The mink coat that my husband bought me at the Salvation Army matches my mittens.

The woman who met me at the bus station was carrying a sign with my name on it—misspelled.

thaw

Just *thaw* your meat. Don't *dethaw* it or *unthaw* it. Neither of those are standard words, and both sound like they mean the opposite of what you probably intend. (*Unthawing* should mean refreezing.) *Thaw* means to unfreeze; to heat up so the object is no longer in a frozen state.

I thought I thawed that possum meat for tacos.

their/there/they're

I just don't get what's so difficult about these words. Yet I see sentences like "Their the ones who did it" all the time. *Their* tells who owns or possesses something. (Whose house is it? It's theirs.) *There* is what you use when you're talking about a place. (We're going there for dessert.) *They're* is short for *they are*. (They're going to the movies.)

The plastic gnomes that were on their front lawn are being held for ransom.

The gnomes aren't there anymore; in their place is a note that says "Leave $100 or the gnomes get blown to smithereens."

They're not going to make it to their flight if they don't quit playing Twister on the airport's people mover.

then *see* **than**

throes/throws

You may be in the *throes* of passion, but you're never in the *throws* of it (unless passion has been throwing you around). Being *in the throes of* something means you're in its clutches. Except in the phrase *throes of passion*, it's usually used to describe something negative; it means you're caught up in a strain or difficulty. I'm not going to patronize you and define *throws*. You already know darn well what that means.

Ken was in the throes of despair after his wife left him for the milkman.

Petra throws the ball to her bulldog, Pansy.

throughfare/thoroughfare
Although there's no such standard word as *throughfare*, writer Steve Circeo complains that he sees street signs in Albuquerque that say "no throughfare." The correct word is *thoroughfare*, which means a public road or other means of travel.

If you want to avoid heavily trafficked thoroughfares, you can take side streets to get to my house; just watch out for those crazy soccer moms.

till
You don't need an apostrophe before the word *till* when you're using it to mean *until*. Believe it or not, *till* is not a shortened form of *until*; the word *till* came first, and the prefix *un-* was added to it later! You can also *till* soil; that means getting it ready for a planting season. And *till* is a British word for a cash register.

I'll love you till dogs can read.
We tilled our land before we planted tomato seeds.

tolerance
I always cringe when teachers talk about "teaching tolerance." Do we really want to teach our kids to "put up with" people of other races, religions, levels of disability, and so on? Are our

kids so horrible that they even *have* to be taught just to do that much? When you *tolerate* someone, it doesn't mean you like that person in any way. In fact, it usually means just the opposite—that you don't like the person, but you have to deal with him. I say we should be aiming for loftier goals. No matter what dictionaries say, I think *tolerance* carries too much of a negative ring to be truly useful in this context.

I have to tolerate my husband's uncle, even when he tells stories about all the women he's "scored with," because he's a member of the family.

tony

Ever since Dominick Dunne started tossing this word around, it's been the new "in" word. So you should probably know what it means: posh, refined, or of the upper crust. However, it's almost never used without an air of sarcasm; its connotation is "snooty" or "hoity-toity."

The celebrity seemed so down-to-earth in front of the cameras; I was disappointed to find out how tony she really is.

torrent

A *torrent* is a lot; an unrestrained flood of something. It's also a quick-moving stream.

She tried to explain her symptoms through a torrent of tears until she got the hiccups and swallowed the thermometer.

torrid

Torrid weather is swelteringly hot. *Torrid* also describes something that's volatile, or invokes passion or other strong feelings.

I had a torrid affair with the mailman.

tortuous/torturous

Twists and turns or a high level of complication make something *tortuous*. Something *torturous* causes or relates to torture, or is horrid or excruciating.

We braved the tortuous road trip over the river and through the woods to Grandmother's house.

I barely completed the torturous physical endurance test for a chance to be on Survivor.

toward/towards

Doesn't matter which one you use, as long as you remain consistent within a piece of writing. Just pick one and stick to it. In journalism, where letters count, writer Mary J. Schirmer notes that it's always *toward*. They both mean in the direction of, close to, regarding, or to be used for.

Walk toward (towards) the cow pasture, but don't step in anything soft and brown.

transgender/transsexual

According to popular usage, *transgender* applies to anyone

whose gender expression doesn't fit with societal expectations for the sex the person was born with. *Transsexual* applies to those who feel they were born "the wrong sex." Transsexuals are sometimes lumped into categories: *post-surgical, presurgical,* and *nonsurgical; post-surgical* meaning that the person has undergone sexual reassignment surgery (SRS), *presurgical* meaning that the person plans to go for surgery, and *nonsurgical* meaning that the person does not plan to have surgery. Note that transgender and transsexual are not descriptions of sexual orientation—transsexuals and transgendered people may be homosexual, heterosexual, or any other sexual variation. Writer Christine Beatty (*www.glamazon.net*) says, "Some people, most of them transsexuals, often bristle at the word *transgender* when applied to them. They reject the way that it is often used—politically—as an umbrella term that covers the full gender gamut from cross-dressers to post-surgical transsexuals to those in between. And I fully defend the right of anybody not to accept any label with which they are uncomfortable or disagree with. On the other hand many transsexuals, myself included, are not particularly threatened by the Big Tent concept."

Edna is an eighty-year-old transgendered woman who prefers to dress in tuxedos.

As a presurgical transsexual, Oliver was saving his lawn-mowing money for sexual reassignment surgery.

transpire

There's a bit of a controversy surrounding *transpire*. You probably know it as a synonym for *occur*, as in "What transpired that day was unacceptable." Well, some grammarians aren't too thrilled with that usage. They complain about it for two reasons: First, it sounds like a pompous substitute for the more common words that can replace it *(occur, happen, take place)*, and second, it doesn't fit the word's etymology. The Latin *trans* (through) and *spirare* (breathe) formed the French word *transpirer*. In English, *transpire* first meant to secrete waste products as a vapor or liquid from a living thing's skin or surface. Figuratively, it came to mean leak out, as in truth that becomes revealed over the course of time. Even though its use as a synonym for *occur* is nearly as long-standing, you may want to avoid using it this way.

It transpired that Buffy actually did have breast enlargement surgery, despite her protestations to the contrary.

traveled *see* **canceled**

troop/troupe

Troupe is only used of performers—you might have an acting, dancing, or musical troupe. *Troop* is the word for military or civilian groups. To *troop* is to travel (usually by foot) in a group. When you want to compliment someone about enduring hardships, the word is *trouper* ("She's a real trouper for putting up with all those screaming kids"). That state police officer who pulls you over for making a rolling stop is a *trooper*, and I bet you can think of some other names for him as well.

I auditioned for an a cappella yodeling troupe in college.

The kids trooped out of the classroom and into the school multipurpose room to watch a documentary about the history of badgers.

trustworthiness
In an August 30, 2000 online interview at CNN.com, President George W. Bush said, "Well, I think if you say you're going to do something and don't do it, that's trustworthiness." Really? I think if you say you're going to do something and don't, that's the opposite of trustworthiness: untrustworthiness. *Trustworthiness* is the quality of warranting trust.

Jean proved her trustworthiness when she showed up on time every day to baby-sit Edgar, my pet crocodile.

T-shirt/tee shirt
It's properly termed a *T-shirt* because it sort of looks like the letter "T" when it's laid flat.

Tony refuses to throw out that old, ragged T-shirt.

turbid/turgid

Turbid is used to describe liquids (usually bodies of water) that are not clear, but rather, cloudy or murky. It can also be used to describe something that is lacking in clarity, or air that's heavily polluted or foggy. If someone says your writing style is *turgid*, it's overly pompous or rife with decorative language that serves no real purpose. In medical terms, *turgid* also means enlarged because of fluid retention.

It's hard to spot the Loch Ness monster in turbid waters.

The turgid writer can never write, "The sun rose." Oh, no. He writes, "The luminescent orb of incandescent gas peeked over the horizon to triumphantly make its debut."

turpitude

It looks like an innocent enough word, but you don't want to be accused of *turpitude*, which means immorality or a heinously disgusting and wrongful act or idea.

Videotaping his roommate in the shower without her consent was a turpitude she can't forgive, even though he agreed to split the reality show pay with her.

Uu

ubiquitous

Ubiquitous means always around, or existing everywhere. Sometimes celebrities are described as *ubiquitous*, meaning that they never really disappear from the public's eye—they seem to be everywhere.

In spring, hand-holding lovers are as ubiquitous as daffodils. In fall, divorce papers are as ubiquitous as colored leaves.

unbelievable

Something is *unbelievable* only if it's so unlikely that you have a very difficult time believing it. "On a dozen cable TV channels most any NBA night, you might hear a Vince Carter dunk described as *unbelievable*. Nah. Believe it, you talking heads," says writer Hubert Mizell in the *St. Petersburg Times*. "Even if Carter does a 360 reverse with eyes shut, he is a talent who constantly flies, contorts, and crams basketballs through hoops. So, not unbelievable. Danny DeVito dunking, now that would be unbelievable."

It's unbelievable that Tracy speaks seven languages, including Klingon, at the age of eight.

unctuous *see* **sycophantic**

undoubtably
Undoubtably is not a standard word. The correct word is *undoubtedly*. But undoubtedly, you knew that, right? Same with *supposably* (which is really *supposedly*).

Irene is undoubtedly the tallest girl in her class; she can read a textbook balanced on the head of her best friend, Myrtle.

unequivocal *see* **ambiguous**

uninterested *see* **disinterested**

unique
In my high school yearbook, right next to "Best Looking" and "Most Likely To Succeed," we had "Most Unique." *Unique* is sort of like *pregnant;* you either are or you aren't. Writer Eunice K. Riemer says, "The word means 'one of a kind, the only one like it in the world,' so one cannot say

something is 'more unique.' What most people mean when they use this description is 'more unusual.' 'More nearly unique' is also possible, although hardly ever encountered in conversation. All this applies to other nouns and adjectives that describe a perfected state. A circle is a certain plane figure, so 'a perfect circle' is redundant and 'more circular' is wrong."

Karen's unique view of the world is apparent in her paintings, where everything is neon green with orange polka dots and no creature or person has eyes.

us/we

Whenever you have a phrase in which you're not sure whether to use *us* or *we*, cross out the next word. For example, if you want to know whether the sentence "We musicians are more sensitive than other people" or "Us musicians are more sensitive than other people" is correct, remove the word *musicians*. Now your sentence possibilities are "We are more sensitive than other people" or "Us are more sensitive than other people." Now doesn't it seem obvious which word to choose?

We secretaries know our bosses would be lost without us.
Rock stars couldn't function without us bathroom attendants.

Vv

vain/vein

Both of these words have a few meanings, so be patient with me. If something's *done in vain*, it doesn't achieve what it was supposed to achieve, or it's pointless. *Vain* also means in love with the mirror; narcissistic or egotistical. You'll also see *vain* in the phrase "take God's name in vain," which means to use His name in a trivial or derogatory way. *Veins* are those things that terribly protrude from your hands (wait, maybe that's just me), and a *vein* is also a genre, style, characteristic, mood, or manner. Leaves and insect wings also have *veins*.

I made a vain attempt to quit eating doughnuts; they just seem to jump into my mouth and demand to be eaten.

Even though Archie assured Rosemary that he'd made the comment about her being on steroids in a humorous vein, she held his car over her head until he took back his words.

vein *also see* **artery**

verbal *see* **oral**

veritable/virtual

If something is *virtual*, it doesn't actually exist. It's either a fantasy, or it's not factually correct, but only nearly so. Writer Lawrence Benedict says, "The latest misuse of the word occurred for me when I had created this great spread of dishes, getting ready for some guests. A friend passed through the room, looked at all the food and said, 'Wow, that's a virtual feast!' (I did not take offense)." The word this guest probably should have used was *veritable*—meaning true.

The musical recording was so good that the singer was virtually in my living room.

I have a veritable collection of unpaid bills; even though I've bribed the mailman to make them stop, he keeps bringing them anyway.

vernacular

Vernacular is slang or words/expressions that are idiosyncratic to a particular group of people (people who are in the same geographic area, same trade, same club, and so forth), or the speech used by the masses rather than the literary elite. Rarely, *vernacular* can be used to describe something other than speech; for example, a custom or style of architecture that exists in a particular region.

The vernacular language in Brooklyn is often hard for a Southerner to understand.

In the vernacular of public health administrators, to be called a nurse is an insult.

via

The preferred definition for *via* is by way of, not by means of. This means it's perfectly acceptable for you to say you got to the mall via the highway, but less acceptable for you to say you sent something via e-mail. (Just use the word *by*.)

I went to Bay Shore via Southern State Parkway.

viable

This may just be a pet peeve, but I don't like it when *viable* is used to describe nonliving things. Etymologically speaking, *viable* comes from the French *vie* (life), which comes from the Latin *vita* (also life). So, doesn't it make sense that it should apply to living things alone? Anyway, *viable* means capable of living. Your business was never capable of being alive in the first place, so don't talk about how viable it is. Instead, you might say it's promising or potentially successful.

My neighbor Brenda wasn't sure how viable her goldfish was after her son Timmy taught it to swim in his glass of orange juice.

vice/vise

Your *vices* are your bad habits or behaviors—sometimes used lightly (nail biting is a vice), and sometimes used very seriously (pedophilia is a vice). The tool that screws together to clamp something down is a *vise*.

Chewing your toenails is a disgusting vice.
Put the wood in a vise so we can drill a hole in it.

vintage

Vintage doesn't just mean old. It refers to the year a wine was made, or is meant as a compliment about something's lasting worthiness or quality.

The vintage song continues to be played on the radio even though it was written fifty years ago.

virtual *see* veritable

viscous

Viscous means viscid. What? That doesn't help? Oh, okay, fine. They both mean having a thick or tacky consistency, or having a hindered flow.

If you'd ever look at the viscous goo that eventually becomes meringue, you might not find it so delectable.

vise *see* vice

vital

Go back three entries and read my little rant about *viable*. Rinse and repeat. *Vital*, which also comes from the Latin *vita* (life), should be used only when talking about living things. If something is *vital*, it's necessary to life, or relating to life. A person is *vital* if she's lively. Your Palm Pilot is not vital. It's not vital that you have a cell phone. Even your early morning cup of coffee (gack!) is not vital. (Come on, you *can* live without it.) Be careful about using *vital* when *essential* or *necessary* would do.

The veterinarian said it was vital that the dung beetle receive a transfusion, but he wasn't sure where to find a donor in Kansas City.

vocation *see* avocation

Ww

we *see* **us**

wherefore
When Juliet asked, "Wherefore art thou Romeo?" she wasn't asking where he was. She was asking *why* he was . . . why he had to be a Montague when she was a Capulet. That's what *wherefore* means: why.

Wherefore must proper English be so difficult?

which *see* **that**

who *see* **that**

Wicca
Wicca is a pagan religion (meaning nature-oriented, worshiping many gods, and/or not Christian, Jewish, or Muslim). *Wiccans* worship a goddess and her partner, a god, and do not believe in

a devil or hell. Yes, Wiccans do practice witchcraft, but what may interest you is the Wiccan Rede (credo): "An ye harm none, do what ye will" (in other words, you may do as you please as long as it doesn't hurt anyone). Wiccans do *not* endorse the use of magick (see *magick* entry) for harmful intentions. Not all witches consider themselves Wiccans. Both male and female practitioners of Wicca are called *witches*.

You may practice Wicca alone, or you may join a coven.

widow/widower

I always get these two confused. A *widow* is a woman whose husband has died, and a *widower* is a man whose wife has died. In both cases, the person is only considered widowed until he or she remarries (if ever).

The widow dreaded the thought of her first Christmas without her husband.

The widower wasn't sure if he was ready to start dating again, but he bought some condoms as a badge of courage.

woken *see* awakened

World Wide Web *see* Internet

wrack *see* rack

wreak/wreck

Just like *sneak*, the past tense is *wreaked*, not *wrought*. Oddly enough, *wrought* is the secondary choice for the past tense of *work*. This didn't stop a *Newsday* reporter from writing, "Prezant and other doctors have vowed to continue studying illnesses wrought by the disaster." And where havoc is concerned, the phrase is to *wreak havoc*, not to *wreck havoc*. To *wreck* is to destroy or mess up. People don't destroy havoc; they bring it about.

The boys wreaked havoc on the house.

Mrs. Oppermier stood at the doorway and announced, "Your son used a baseball bat to wreck my mailbox."

wretch *see* **retch**

writer *see* **author**

wunderkind

The word is *wunderkind*, not *wonderkid*. I once quoted a literary manager in an international magazine as calling his partner "a wonderkid." This is my penance. There is no such standard word. A *wunderkind* (German for *wonder child*) is a child prodigy; someone who shows unusually high aptitude or great talent at a young age.

Six-year-old Beth's phenomenal skill in mathematics makes her a true wunderkind.

WU...

Yy, Zz

you're/your

Just like *their* and *they're*, *your* and *you're* get mixed up, too. And not just by dunderheads, either. Consider this example, written by Thomas Clark, the former editor of *Writer's Digest* magazine, in his book *Queries & Submissions:* "And even if your best pal is an editor, you're queries should still be complete . . ." I don't know how this one made it past the book's copyeditor. "You are queries should still be complete?" I think not. *Your* shows possession: Whose hat is that? It's *your* hat. Whose queries should be complete? *Your* queries. *You're* is a contraction for *you are*.

Your dog is terrorizing my cat again.

You're not really going to wrap your Christmas gifts in newspaper, are you?

zenith *see* **nadir**

Phrases

Aa

A.D./B.C.
Although some people remember it as "after death," *A.D.* stands for *anno Domini*, which means *in the year of the Lord*, or *in the year of our Lord*. It belongs before the year (A.D. 2004). *B.C.* stands for *before Christ*, and it belongs after the year (600 B.C.).

I was born in A.D. 1975.

Sumerians started to use fillings in cavities around 3000 B.C., and yet my dentist still can't figure out how to fill my teeth without sending me through the roof in pain.

ATM machine
Because *ATM* stands for *automated teller machine*, "ATM machine" is redundant.

I had to go to the ATM six times while I was Christmas shopping on Tuesday.

ad hoc

Ad hoc is Latin for "to this." If it's *ad hoc*, it only applies to the case or situation being addressed. An ad hoc group is formed for one purpose, and then usually breaks up. *Ad hoc* can also mean thought up on the fly.

Kermit formed an ad hoc group of Muppets to campaign for their favorite political candidate, Fozzy Bear.

ad hominem

Ad hominem literally means "to the person." It's a personal attack—one that attempts to discredit a person's ideas, arguments, or positions by insulting the person himself or herself.

"You can't trust a word Laura says because she wears so much lipstick she looks like she's been making out with a tomato" is ad hominem.

aiding and abedding/aiding and abetting

Unless you're helping and making up someone's bed, you're *aiding and abetting*. To *abet* is to help someone, and it carries the connotation of doing something against the law or morally wrong. So, yes, it's kind of a redundant phrase—both aid and abet do mean to help. Oh, and you think I'm kidding about people misusing this phrase? My last search of Google turned up fifty-seven Web sites in which people had used the phrase "aiding and abedding."

John Frances was caught aiding and abetting the kids who stole the school mascot.

anchors away/anchors aweigh

The correct expression is *anchors aweigh*, which means you're pulling up the anchor so it's no longer on the sea bottom.

When the alcoholic captain yelled, "Anchors aweigh!" the first mate stared at him because the ship was on a hoist in dry dock.

angels on the head of a pin/angels on the point of a needle

The correct expression is, "How many angels can dance on the point of a very fine needle?" The earliest use of this question that I could find comes from Isaac D'Israeli's *Curiosities of Literature*, 1791–1834: "The reader desirous of being merry with Aquinas's angels may find them in Martinus Scriblerus, in Ch. VII, who inquires if angels pass from one extreme to another without going through the middle? And if angels know things more clearly in a morning? How many angels can dance on the point of a very fine needle, without jostling one another?"

another thing coming/another think coming

Here's one I didn't know until I started researching this book. I would have sworn that there was nothing wrong with *another thing coming*, but I would have been wrong. The correct expression is the somewhat ungrammatical *another think coming*, as in, "If that's what you think, you have another think coming."

Irene told her daughter, "Joanie, if you think I'm going to drive a forty-three-year-old woman to a rave, you have another think coming. And change that dress—it's too tight."

Bb

bald-faced/bold-faced

Bald-faced is correct. It means obvious; without any mask or covering. You'll usually see it in the phrase *bald-faced lie*.

When eight-month-pregnant Marcia told her mother she was still a virgin, that was a bald-faced lie.

barbed wire/bob wire

I fully realize that the Backstreet Boys are not expected to be paragons of literacy, but I just heard Howie Dorough talk about fans who climbed a *bob wire* fence to get to the group. Good thing the boy can sing. It's *barbed wire*.

Barbed wire fence surrounds the prison, the warden explained, to keep out the fans of the rapper inmates.

begs the question

Here's one of the most misused phrases of all time, and I vote that we ban this expression altogether, because even if

be...

you use it correctly, most people won't know what you mean. Journalists often say that something *begs the question* when they mean that there's a question begging to be asked. A celebrity says, "I'm seriously involved with someone," and a journalist says, "Well, that just *begs the question*—are you engaged?" Wrong. To *beg the question* is to offer as proof something that itself hasn't been proved; for example, "Women shouldn't be allowed to vote because men are better decision-makers." It may also use the original thing that needs to be proved as part (or all) of the argument: "Tall people are smarter because you have to be intelligent to be tall" is *begging the question.*

being that

Being that is a nonstandard way of saying *because.* ("Being that she was sick, she didn't go out.) Eliminate this phrase from your writing. Stick to *because.*

between you and I/between you and me

Even certain unnamed presidents have thought it sounded better to say *between you and I,* but the correct grammar is *between you and me.*

Between you and me, I think John is sexy when he slicks his hair back with shortening.

black comedy

Also known as dark comedy, a *black comedy* is a film that takes serious subject matter and addresses it in a humorous fashion, even when it may seem inappropriate. It has nothing to do with the race of the actors or filmmakers. Examples of black comedies include *Better Off Dead* (dealing with suicide), *The Cable Guy* (dealing with stalking), *Heathers* (dealing with murder), and *Pulp Fiction* (dealing with drug overdoses, murder, and armed robbery).

If Herbert wanted Louise to go with him to see a black comedy, he had to promise not to set fire to the popcorn tub again.

bob wire *see* barbed wire

Bob's your uncle

Bob's your uncle means you have a lock on it, you'll attain it easily, or "no problem." The phrase seems to come from an incident in which British Prime Minister Lord Robert Marquis of Salisbury appointed his own nephew (Arthur Balfour) Chief Secretary for Ireland in 1887. Since "Bob" had already given Arthur other high positions, people decided Arthur had it easy because Bob was his uncle.

Just fill out this paperwork for a loan with a 50 percent annual interest rate, and—Bob's your uncle—you'll be approved for credit.

bold-faced *see* **bald-faced**

bon mot

In French, *bon mot* means good word. In English, we use it to refer to a clever—often biting—one-liner.

Comedian Rodney Dangerfield is known for his bons mots about getting no respect.

bona fide

In Latin, *bona fide* means in good faith. We use it to mean genuine—you'll most often hear it in the phrase *a bona fide offer,* meaning that the offer isn't being made lightly or as a "test," but rather that the offer is serious.

I'm making you a bona fide offer to buy your llama.

bull session

A *bull session* is a group chat. According to the "Sayings and Everyday Expressions" Web site (*www.geocities.com/ronboy. geo/index.html*), it is so named because bulls tend to bellow back and forth at each other when they are stuck in a pen together.

The women's quilting group held a bull session to discuss the most effective methods of birth control, using items commonly found in any kitchen.

Cc

carpe diem

In case you missed the movie *Dead Poets Society*, *carpe diem* is Latin for *seize the day*. Good advice, don't you think?

"Stop worrying about what the future holds," the chemistry professor told his students as he prepared to demonstrate a hydrogen bomb, "and carpe diem!"

champ at the bit/chomp at the bit

This is kind of a funny one, because *champing* does mean repeatedly chomping. Some animals *champ* (open and close their mouths, making a chomping noise) as part of a mating ritual. The correct expression is *champ at the bit* when you mean to say that someone is eager or excited.

Old Willie McGee was champing at the bit to hear his first recorded song, "All the Wheat in Oklahoma Couldn't Get Me to Eat Your Cornbread," on his hometown radio station.

could care less/couldn't care less

This one drives me bananas. If you *could care less*, that means you do care, at least a little—because it's possible for you to care less. If you didn't care at all, then you *couldn't care less*.

I couldn't care less if you tattooed my name on your forehead; I'm still not going out with you.

could of and should of/could have and should have

Probably because of the way the contractions (*could've* and *should've*) sound, these phrases have been abused. The correct expressions are *could have* and *should have*. Toss the *of*. It just ain't right.

I could have told you not to call your ex-boyfriend while you were drunk, but it was fun to watch you beg him to take you back.

I should have popped the balloons instead of letting the kids suck all the helium out of them.

cutting off your nose despite your face/cutting off your nose to spite your face

Cutting off your nose to spite your face is the correct expression. You're cutting off your nose just to vex the rest of your face. It refers to times when a person isn't looking at the big picture.

If you don't cash your income tax refund check just because you don't like the government's welfare reform policy, you're cutting off your nose to spite your face.

Dd

de jure/de facto

De jure is rightful and lawful; *de facto* is in fact (actual). A *de facto* government is the one that's in power, even if they didn't get there legally. A *de jure* one has rightful claim to their power.

Despite Hildy's efforts to exercise de jure power as organizer of the Tuesday Canasta Club bake sale, the deranged de facto president outlawed cherry crumb coffee cakes anyway.

deep-seated/deep-seeded

Deep-seated is correct—it refers to how deeply something is set.

Because of Albert's deep-seated fear of dentists, he now has to gum all of his food.

déjà vu

Déjà vu is a French phrase that means "already seen." It is appropriate only when you feel like you've experienced something before, but in reality, you're experiencing it for the first time.

When I visited the Eiffel Tower for the first time, I had a profound sense of déjà vu.

different from/different than

The correct expression is *different from*, not *different than*. "His taste in music is different than mine" is wrong.

The color of his toupee is different from the color of his beard.

dire straights/dire straits

When you're terribly down on your luck, you're in *dire straits*, not *dire straights*. A *strait* is a very narrow passageway that joins two bodies of water, or a distressing situation. Think of it this way: When you're in *dire straits*, you're walking a very thin line.

I was in dire straits after I got pregnant, because I couldn't decide which boyfriend to blame.

dog-eat-dog world/doggy-dog world

I have to hold back a laugh when someone uses this one wrong. It may be a *dog-eat-dog world*, but it's not a *doggy-dog world* (except maybe at the dog shows).

I'm not surprised to hear that Miss Georgia ripped runs in all of Miss New Jersey's pantyhose; it's a dog-eat-dog world.

due to

Never start a sentence with "due to," or let it come right after a comma. ("Due to your help" and "The bake sale, due to your help, sold out" are both wrong.) The phrase *due to* must have a linking verb and it must be attached to a noun.

Our bake sale's success is due to the work of our publicity director.

Dutch auction

According to eBay, a Dutch auction "features multiple quantities of an item. All winning bidders pay the same price—the lowest successful bid at the end of the auction." According to the *American Heritage Dictionary*, a Dutch auction is one in which an item starts out by being offered at a high price, and then comes down in increments until someone bids. You decide who you want to believe.

Fritz bought eight pairs of wooden shoes at an online Dutch auction, at $2 a pair.

Ee

e.g./i.e.
One of my teachers, who will remain nameless (you'd think this was to protect her innocence, but the truth is that I just can't remember which teacher it was—oh, I'd name her otherwise; I'm cruel like that), once taught me that *i.e.* was short for "in example." She lied, and I went on to use *i.e.* improperly for the next decade or so. It's actually an abbreviation of the Latin *id est*, which means "that is." *E.g.* stands for the Latin *exempli gratia*, which means "for example." Both need to be followed by commas.

Sure, you could be a television star; I'm sure there are many shows that would love to have you appear (e.g., Jerry Springer and Ricki Lake).

He's a waste removal expert (i.e., a garbageman).

ex post facto
The Latin *ex post facto* means after the fact. You'll usually hear about it in legal terms; it's not legal for someone to be tried for

a crime if the law was instated after the crime took place (*ex post facto*).

Leonard can't be tried for stalking because anti-stalking laws were passed ex post facto.

exception proves the rule
In today's terminology, it isn't possible for an exception to prove a rule. The German *prüfen* means to test, and so does the Latin *probare*. Allegedly, that's what the expression really means: The exception tests the rule. In this manner, *proves* could be substituted for *proofs* (which means to check for mistakes; test for accuracy). At least that makes some sense, but there is disagreement among scholars about this explanation; some believe its true meaning is more like, "the exception proves that there *is* a rule," and some believe it never made any sense to begin with. I vote to toss it altogether.

Ff

feel badly

Go ahead and *feel bad* if you must, but don't *feel badly*. Because the adverb (*badly*) modifies the verb (*feeling*), *feeling badly* means that your sense of touch is bad, or that your emotions aren't working correctly . . . rare afflictions, indeed.

> *I can't check for lumps in your breasts today; I am feeling badly.*

feet of clay

This expression means that the subject has a fault and is usually used to describe someone who appeared to be perfect or beyond criticism. In the biblical Book of Daniel (2:31–33), Daniel explains that the king had a dream about a statue; the head was gold, the breast and arms were silver, belly and thighs were brass, and legs were iron, but the feet were part iron and part clay. Daniel predicts that just as clay is easily broken, the kingdom will fall apart as well.

When Dina told us she had a gambling problem, I was shocked to realize that my idol had feet of clay.

first cousin once removed/second cousin
Okay, you know who your cousins are. They're the children of your aunts and uncles. But do you know who your *first cousins once removed* are? They're your cousin's children and your parents' cousins. Your *second cousins* are your parents' cousins' children.

for all intensive purposes/for all intents and purposes
Even though it's a redundant expression, *for all intents and purposes* is correct.

For all intents and purposes, this contract to drill an oil well in my front yard will suffice.

forbidden from/forbidden to
Forbid is always followed by *to*, not *from*. When a mom tells her grounded son, "You are forbidden from going out tonight," if the son is cheeky, he might correct her English.

Because I'm lactose-intolerant, I am forbidden to eat ice cream.

Gg

genuine faux

Now there's a paradox if I ever saw one. I have to forcibly stop myself from banging my head against a wall when I see a couch marked "genuine faux leather." Would you say it was "real fake leather"? *Faux* is the French word for false. Faux pearls are imitation pearls. *Faux* is not a selling point!

graduate college/graduate from college

No matter how good your grades are, you can't *graduate college*. You can only *graduate from college*, or the college can graduate you. You are the object that will be graduated; the college isn't being graduated.

Boston University graduated me in 1997.

Arlene graduated from the Mohawk Hairstyle Academy in the bottom 5 percent of her class.

ground zero

After the attacks of September 11, 2001, I heard the words *ground zero* at least a hundred times before I bothered to look them up. *Ground zero* has four meanings: the site of a nuclear attack, the site of brutal destruction or frenzy, the site of massive growth or change, or the starting point. The World Trade Center could fit with two of those definitions: It was the site of tremendous destruction, and it was demolished until it was back to its starting point.

When the newlyweds' home slid down the hill into the creek bed, they were back to ground zero.

Hh

hairbrained/hare-brained
Come on, now, *hairs* don't have brains. *Hares* (wild rabbits) do, however—small though their brains may be. A *hare-brained idea* is an ill-conceived one.

His hare-brained plan to invent a self-cleaning refrigerator will never work.

half-mast/half-staff
A flag is only at *half-mast* if it's on a ship or at a naval station. Otherwise, it's at *half-staff*.

happy median/happy medium
The correct phrase is *happy medium*, even though I think *happy median* makes more sense! You've struck a happy medium when you've found a satisfactory balance between two extremes.

You want to go to California and I want to go to Florida—maybe Texas would be a happy medium?

hara-kiri

Two surprises about this phrase. First, it's spelled and pronounced *hara-kiri*, not *hari-kari*. Second, it doesn't just refer to any suicide; it specifically refers to suicide by disembowelment. (Yuck!) In Japanese, *hara* means abdomen and *kiri* means to cut.

The soldier took out his sharpest knife and was about to commit hara-kiri when the chef announced there would be pizza for dinner, which made the soldier change his mind.

here, here; hear, hear

This is another one I was never too sure about. I sometimes liked to mix it up to *hear, here*, just so I'd be sure I had at least one word correct. The proper expression is *hear, hear*, and it's short for *hear him, hear him*—as in, listen to him (or her). It's used to express endorsement.

After Biff said that we should install a mechanical bull in the coffee break room, I shouted, "Hear, hear!"

hoi polloi

If you had to wager a guess, would you say *hoi polloi* described rich and sophisticated people (the elite), or common people (the masses)? If you said "common people," I'm impressed. That's what it means, but probably because it sounds like *hoity-toity*, people often think it means the opposite.

I think your scholarly book is too arcane for the hoi polloi.

i.e. *see* **e.g.**

if I was/if I were
"If I were a rich man, . . ." Remember *Fiddler on the Roof*? That's all you have to remember if you're unsure of whether to use *was* or *were* with *if I*. Even though *I* is singular, it takes the subjunctive form. The correct phrase is *if I were*.

If I were you, I'd try to whip up some tears to get out of the traffic ticket.

ipso facto
Ipso facto means "by that fact."

A man, by the fact that he is a man, can't bear children; therefore, a man, ipso facto, can't bear children.

A child, ipso facto, is not allowed to buy alcohol.

Jj

je ne sais quoi

In French, *je ne sais quoi* means "I don't know what." If a person has a certain *je ne sais quoi*, he has a personal magnetism or a special, indescribable quality.

I'm not sure what it is that attracts me to that painting; it just has that je ne sais quoi.

jerry-built/jury-rigged

"*Jury-rigged* usually gets mangled into *jerry rigged*," says Cynthia Amorese. "*Jury-rigged* means improvising with what's available to deal with an emergency or immediate need. This is what people who use *jerry rigged* usually mean, but the *jerry* word is really *jerry-built*, which means cheap, shoddy workmanship."

He jury-rigged the muffler by wrapping a wire hanger around it.

The jerry-built bookshelves collapsed under the weight of my magazine collection.

jump-start/jumpstart

Lately, I've been on a mission to give the hyphen its rightful place. There are so many poor unemployed hyphens; won't you give one a job so it can feed its family? It belongs in *jump-start*. I don't care what anyone else says. (Save the hyphens!)

After a slow season, I need to jump-start my writing sales.

just deserts/just desserts

Unless the evil people are getting Boston cream pies, they're not getting their *just desserts*. They're getting what they deserve; their *just deserts*. In this case, *desert* means something that is warranted or deserved.

I love movies where the villain gets his just deserts.

Kk

kitten caboodle/kit and caboodle
Blahahaha! I can't believe I'm even giving this one the satisfaction of seeing itself in print, but kittens don't have caboodles. The *whole kit and caboodle* means the whole thing; the whole ball of wax. I think the *doggy-dog world* people should be forced to marry the *kitten caboodle* people, and they should be immediately sterilized.

Ll

leave alone/let alone

Leave alone means to make someone be by himself or herself. *Let alone* means not to mess with something. People tend to use *leave alone* for both meanings, as in this exchange: "Should I add more garlic to the sauce?" asked Sonia. "Leave it alone! It's perfect," said Phil. In this case, Phil doesn't mean that Sonia should leave the room so the sauce is by itself. He means that she shouldn't do anything to it—let it alone.

I left Kyle alone so he could contemplate why it was wrong to put a frog in Stephanie's locker.

Quit trying to reload the Web page and just let it alone.

light years

Light years is a measure of distance, not time—so there's no such thing as *light years ago* or *light years from now.* A light year is almost six trillion miles.

Even though we moved only to the next state, we feel like we're light years away from our family in Missouri.

Mm

mano a mano
In Spanish, *mano a mano* means hand to hand, not man to man. If someone challenges you to fight *mano a mano*, you won't be using any weapons.

Let's settle this fight mano a mano.

mother load/mother lode
Lode means an ore deposit or riches, so the correct expression when you mean you've hit the source of something plentiful or valuable is *mother lode*.

You hit the mother lode when you started selling your see-through bikinis by infomercial.

mo...

Nn

near miss

If you had a *near miss*, then you had the accident (but just barely); if you *nearly* missed something, you didn't miss it. That's probably not what you mean. You probably mean you had a close call, or a near accident.

    My car had a near miss with a fire hydrant, and I almost fainted when I got the repair bill from the city.

new development

This is redundant. Developments are, by definition, new.

    There has been a development in the case of the rooster who broke into the chicken coop.

no thanks/no, thanks

No thanks means there is an absence of gratitude. *No, thanks* is what to use when you want to decline politely. Remember the comma.

    "Would you like frogs' legs?" "No, thanks."

    I got no thanks for putting potpourri in my boyfriend's sock drawer.

Oo

off of

I made the gaffe of offering "50% off of our already reduced prices" at my Web site. You don't need the word *of* after *off*. I should have offered "50% off our already reduced prices."

I fell off the ladder and plopped right into the paint bucket.

oh, la, la

French people laugh at us for the way we draw out "oooh, la, la!" We exaggerate our pronunciation of it, and most of us suppose that's just the way French people do it. Actually, they say it like it's all one quick word—"ohlala," with the emphasis on the *oh* (not pronounced "ooh").

Did the boss really overhear you calling him a blowhard? Oh, la, la.

old adage

Another redundancy. An *adage* is, by definition, an old saying.

"When all else fails, read the directions" was my father's adage for assembling toys on Christmas Eve.

Old English

"People mistakenly say *Old English* when referring to the language contained in Shakespeare's plays," says writer LeAnn R. Ralph. "Technically, of course, it's Middle English. We can read Shakespeare. Maybe not without difficulty for some, but we can read it. Old English is a language that sounds like German and has some really weird symbols in it for letters. The average person who can read English wouldn't be able to decipher Old English."

Old English was the language in England before A.D. 1100; of course, it wasn't old to them.

on the lam/on the lamb

If you're on the run, you're *on the lam*, assuming you're not riding the back of a lamb while trying to escape. Lambs make poor getaway vehicles, so this will probably never be the case.

The person who stole the motel sign is on the lam.

once and a while/once in a while

I don't understand how this one got mangled. The correct saying is, of course, *once in a while. Once and a while* doesn't make any sense.

I like to see a Broadway show once in a while, whenever I can get the lady next door to watch my mule.

one of the only
Bad phrase. Either it's *one of the few*, or it's *the only*, but it can't be *one of the only*, since there can be only one *only*. (Did I just make your head spin?)

Colleen is one of the few cheerleaders on the squad who can toss a baton the length of the football field.

Her twin sister, Maureen, is the only girl on the squad who can catch that twirling baton in her teeth.

out-of-body/outer body
The correct expression is an *out-of-body experience* to describe the feeling that you are not in your own body, but are watching yourself from another perspective.

Allen claims to have had an out-of-body experience after his heart attack at the bar; he swears he was hovering over the pool table watching Bubba and Bullet throw beer in his face to try to revive him.

Pp, Rr

per diem
Latin for "per day," *per diem* has come to mean the budget granted for daily expenses. When someone offers you a *per diem*, he's offering you a set amount of money that you can spend on food, lodging, gas, and so on.

I got a $100 per diem when I worked on the movie set, but that wasn't enough to cover meals and nightclubs, so I fasted that week.

PIN number
PIN stands for *personal identification number*, so *PIN number* is redundant.

Sister Mary Theophila couldn't place her weekly bet with the bookie at the dry cleaner's because she couldn't remember the PIN for the convent's debit card.

proof is in the pudding/proof of the pudding is in the eati

The correct expression, which dates back to about 1600, "The proof of the pudding is in the eating." In this case, *proof* means test (just as *prove* may mean test in "the exception proves the rule"). You can sum up the meaning as, "wait for the results before passing judgment."

I know Valerie says she can quit maxing out her credit cards, but the proof of the pudding is in the eating.

reason is because

The word *reason* and the word *because* convey the same meaning; therefore, you don't need to say them both together. Even worse, some people say "the reason why is because." In that case, *reason*, *why*, and *because* all mean the same thing. "The reason why I went is because I was hoping a producer would be there" can be shortened to "I went because I was hoping a producer would be there."

The reason I won't marry you is that I'm holding out for someone with a navel.

revert back

Say it with me now: redundant! When you *revert*, you go back.

Spending time with my old friends made me feel like I'd reverted to my high school days, except that back then, everyone had hair, no one was divorced, and we could remember each other's names.

rock 'n' roll
Because you're leaving off both the first and last letter of "and," you need to put apostrophes before and after the remaining "n." You haven't saved any time or space. It's kind of like abbreviating *July* with *Jul.* Why bother?

I like that old-time rock 'n' roll better than I like that crazy rap.

Ss

saps my energy/zaps my energy
In this sense, to *sap* is to deplete, so the correct expression is *saps my energy* (or my patience, or my will to live . . .).

Shopping at the mall with my seventeen-year-old quintuplets really saps my energy.

scot free
The etymology of this expression is questionable. It probably came from the Old English word *sceot*, which meant a tax or penalty, so to get off *scot free* was to get away without paying taxes. But I'm not here to get into a big debate about word origins, so I'll just tell you that the correct spelling is *scot free*, not *Scott free*. Some argue that this expression is an ethnic slam at people from Scotland, who are noted to be frugal.

Amanda Applebaum got off scot free when the stolen lunch money miraculously reappeared on the teacher's desk.

second cousin *see* **first cousin once removed**

senseless murder
A BBC headline reads, "Senseless murder haunts teenage killer." Now you tell me . . . is there any such thing as a *sensible murder*? Same with *untimely death;* whose death is timely?

shoe-in/shoo-in
Maybe the confusion here is because of the expression "get your foot in the door," but if you're a sure thing, then you're a *shoo-in*. The term comes from horse racing, where it's said that corrupt jockeys would *shoo* a particular horse to the finish line to win bets. Which horse would win? The one that was shooed in!

She's a shoo-in for Office Plant Funeral Conductor of the Year.

slush pile
In the publishing and film worlds, a *slush pile* is the lot of unsolicited submissions that writers send in the hopes of getting the works published or produced.

The editor spent her weekend mining the slush pile, hoping to find the next Hope Diamond of a manuscript, or at least a cubic zirconia dazzling enough to convince the publisher to give her some overtime pay.

sour grapes

In the *Aesop's Fables* story of "The Fox and the Grapes," the fox strolls through an orchard and comes upon a bunch of grapes on a vine. Feeling thirsty, he jumps and jumps, but can't quite reach them. He finally gives up and walks away "with his nose in the air, saying: 'I am sure they are sour.'" The moral of the story? "It is easy to despise what you cannot get." *Sour grapes* has nothing to do with envy and everything to do with rationalization.

When you say that you didn't win Miss Photogenic because the photographer used the wrong kind of flash, which made the light bounce off your nose like an airport beacon, that's just sour grapes.

suppose to/supposed to

You were *supposed to* do the dishes. You weren't *suppose to*. Remember the "d"!

I know I'm supposed to be charitable, but you leave me dangling when you borrow my push-up bra.

su....

toe the line/tow the line
Another surprise: the correct expression is *toe the line*. In sports like track, your toe shouldn't be beyond the starting line before the race begins. If you *toe the line*, you're playing by the rules.

I know Uncle Steve would give me a leading role opposite Tom Hanks, but I prefer to toe the line and audition with thousands of other would-be starlets.

try and/try to
It's almost never correct to say *try and*. For example, "I will try and get the work done" is wrong, unless you mean to say that you will try, and you will also get the work done. What you most likely mean is that you will *try to* get the work done.

My New Year's resolution is to try to stop using the phrase "try and."

Uu, Vv

use to/used to
Just like *supposed to*, the correct expression is *used to*, not use to.

I used to wear a retainer, but I accidentally left it on my cafeteria tray and lost it.

veil of tears/vale of tears
A *vale* is a valley; the expression *vale of tears* has come to mean a world full of sorrow. Pretty as it sounds, nix the *veil of tears*—except possibly in the context of the pun used by *USA Today* when they used it to headline a statistic about women crying at weddings.

When my ferret Gladys died, I hoped she was in a better place than in this vale of tears.

vis-à-vis
The *Salaam Morning Daily* contained this sentence: "The U.S. foreign policy vis-à-vis the Iran-Iraq war consisted of four stages." *Vis-à-vis* means face-to-face, not regarding.

I need to speak with you vis-à-vis about my missing bread warmer.

Ww, Zz

well-heeled/well-healed
If you're *well-heeled*, you have plenty of money. If you're *well-healed*, your bronchitis is all gone. Um . . . that was a joke.

His cold sores well-healed, the well-heeled bachelor had an entourage of female admirers.

wet your appetite/whet your appetite
You *whet* someone's appetite, meaning that you entice him. You don't want to pour liquid on anyone's appetite.

Leopold wanted to whet Lucy's appetite for a trip to the Alps, so he welded skis to her wheelchair.

worse comes to worse/worst comes to worst
Use *worst comes to worst* when you reference the worst-case scenario.

If worst comes to worst and it rains on prom night, I'll have to wear a hat.

zaps my energy *see* **saps my energy**

Quiz

Now it's time to test yourself! In the sentences below, a word or phrase may be misused—or the sentence might be fine just the way it is. It's up to you to pick out the incorrectly used words and phrases.

1. Due to our auspicious start, I waited with bated breath to find out if our garage sale would earn us enough money to buy a new television.
   a. Due to
   b. Auspicious
   c. Bated
   d. Sentence is correct as is

2. Even though he demolished the car, I thought his explanation was credulous and not disingenuous.
   a. Demolished
   b. Credulous
   c. Disingenuous
   d. Sentence is correct as is

3. Since he was a little boy, he's had an illogical and deep-seeded prejudice against wunderkind musicians.
   a. Since
   b. Deep-seeded
   c. Wunderkind
   d. Sentence is correct as is

4. I may supplement my income by writing sensual poetry, but I don't think my work arouses prurient interests.
   a. Supplement
   b. Sensual
   c. Prurient
   d. Sentence is correct as is

5. I overheard that the teenager absconded since he was in danger of being arrested on shoplifting charges.
   a. Overheard
   b. Absconded
   c. Since
   d. Sentence is correct as is

6. Alot of people who have chronic allergies are averse to getting allergy shots.
   a. Alot
   b. Chronic
   c. Averse
   d. Sentence is correct as is

7. Jane realized that reading the obituaries section in the newspaper every day was having a pernicious effect on her mood, so now she just peruses it.
   a. Pernicious
   b. Effect
   c. Peruses
   d. Sentence is correct as is

8. I might brutalize you if you bring my doughnuts into the other room; quit trying to cadge my snacks!
   a. Brutalize
   b. Bring
   c. Cadge
   d. Sentence is correct as is

5-8

9. Although it's not in my bailiwick, I wouldn't mind playing billiards with you for awhile.
   a. Bailiwick
   b. Billiards
   c. Awhile
   d. Sentence is correct as is

10. If you hadn't sneaked into the boss's office and stolen his sorbet, you would have been a shoo-in for the promotion.
    a. Sneaked
    b. Sorbet
    c. Shoo-in
    d. Sentence is correct as is

11. Although I am loathe to admit it, I can be loquacious, and sometimes I even use malapropisms.
    a. Loathe
    b. Loquacious
    c. Malapropisms
    d. Sentence is correct as is

12. I am repulsed by your noisome body odor, so don't try to tell me you showered today—I know that's a bald-faced lie.
    a. Repulsed
    b. Noisome
    c. Bald-faced
    d. Sentence is correct as is

13. While poring through the newspaper, I was disturbed by the way the editorial writer pontificated about the causes of the HIV virus.
    a. Poring
    b. Pontificated
    c. HIV virus
    d. Sentence is correct as is
14. He was reticent about why he razed his house to the ground, saying only, "I ought to have done it a long time ago."
    a. Reticent
    b. Razed
    c. Ought
    d. Sentence is correct as is
15. Forbear from launching into a diatribe about political correctness; if my bluntness bothers you, I'll use euphemisms from now on.
    a. Forbear
    b. Diatribe
    c. Euphemisms
    d. Sentence is correct as is
16. If I was having a torrid affair with the pool boy, I'd tell you.
    a. If I was
    b. Torrid
    c. Sentence is correct as is

17. Our nascent little company will make the *Fortune* 500 list—plan on it!
   a. Nascent
   b. Plan on
   c. Sentence is correct as is

18. Just between you and me, I had a strong sense of déjà vu when we first visited Dallas.
   a. Between you and me
   b. Déjà vu
   c. Sentence is correct as is

19. It's vital that you remain stationary so the motion sensors don't go off.
   a. Vital
   b. Stationary
   c. Sentence is correct as is

20. I am sanguine that my wallet won't be robbed while I ride the subways in New York.
   a. Sanguine
   b. Robbed
   c. Sentence is correct as is

21. We don't have to walk much farther; I can't wait for you to see the enormity of the new house!
   a. Farther
   b. Enormity
   c. Sentence is correct as is

22. Although he is reticent to talk about it, he follows a very strict exercise regimen.
    a. Reticent
    b. Regimen
    c. Sentence is correct as is
23. I lay down because I was feeling nauseous.
    a. Lay
    b. Nauseous
    c. Sentence is correct as is
24. The arrogant scholar was apt to imply that he was smarter than the rest of us.
    a. Apt
    b. Imply
    c. Sentence is correct as is
25. I sighted the car careening down the road.
    a. Sighted
    b. Careening
    c. Sentence is correct as is
26. I prevented a large percentage of people from voting for the dishonest politician.
    a. Prevented
    b. Percentage
    c. Sentence is correct as is

22-26

27. Give the dog a dose of antihistamine if it keeps scratching it's rash.
   a. Dose
   b. It's
   c. Sentence is correct as is

28. I think it's hysterical that the boss extolled your hard work; if only he knew you spent most of your work time surfing the Internet for freebies.
   a. Hysterical
   b. Extolled
   c. Sentence is correct as is

29. After running the marathon this fall, my cousin was so exhausted that he was prostrate on the ground for an hour.
   a. Fall
   b. Prostrate
   c. Sentence is correct as is

30. The loquacious stranger told me all about her picayune problems.
   a. Loquacious
   b. Picayune
   c. Sentence is correct as is

Correct or Incorrect?

31. "Your lips are like roses" is a simile.
32. Biweekly means twice a week.
33. Cat litter has an unpleasant aroma.
34. If someone calls you "officious," it means you're getting on his nerves.
35. Bob is John's confidante.
36. In the sentence "Purple horses can't fly," the penultimate word is "fly."
37. If your ski boots irritate your ankles and cause a burn, the skin is chafed.
38. When you zero in on a target, you're homing in.
39. The goggles sunk to the bottom of the pool.
40. Royalty are not part of the hoi polloi.
41. Children are usually anxious to open their birthday presents.
42. When you sing, you're using your vocal chords.
43. If a roadway is blocked, it's impassable.
44. If you have twenty-two apples, then you have over twenty apples.
45. A verbal agreement may be written.
46. Alleviating a problem only lessens it temporarily.
47. You're pouring over your reading material if you're reading it carefully.
48. If something is causing you a lot of stress, it's nerve-wracking.
49. "I'm so excited to see you and I just can't wait for you to come" is an example of a tautology.
50. "Does she sell seashells by the seashore?" is an inquiry.

Answers

1. A	18. C	35. Incorrect
2. B	19. A	36. Incorrect
3. B	20. B	37. Correct
4. D	21. B	38. Correct
5. C	22. A	39. Incorrect
6. A	23. B	40. Correct
7. C	24. C	41. Incorrect
8. B	25. A	42. Incorrect
9. C	26. A	43. Correct
10. D	27. B	44. Incorrect
11. A	28. A	45. Correct
12. A	29. C	46. Correct
13. C	30. C	47. Incorrect
14. B	31. Correct	48. Incorrect
15. D	32. Incorrect	49. Correct
16. A	33. Incorrect	50. Incorrect
17. B	34. Correct	